Praise For

Courage to Live: Learning to Live Again After Loss

Though God tells us clearly in His Word that we, as believers, do not grieve as the world grieves, like people without hope, the reality is that *we do still grieve*. In the pages of **Courage to Live: Learning to Live Again After Loss**, Julie Fillinger testifies in the heart-wrenching pages of her story to the comforting nearness of God as well as the hope He provides in the midst of our deepest valleys.

In 2 Corinthians 1:3-5 we read that when the Lord compassionately ministers to us in our most profound troubles, He equips us to one day comfort others with that same comfort we ourselves received from Him. Needless to say, there is no one better equipped to comfort and encourage you as you journey through the valley of grief and confusion than Julie.

Wendy Speake, author of *The 40 Day Sugar Fast, The 40 Day Feast* and other books

***

In his classic work *The Screwtape Letters,* C.S. Lewis said that "...courage is not simply *one* of the virtues, but the form of every virtue at the testing point." In the pages of this beautifully written book saturated in a faith refined by fire, Julie Fillinger models what courage in the face of trauma looks like. You will discover where the roots of courage are planted, and you will see how one can maintain hope for the long haul of life, whatever twists and turns you may face. As you read her story, as you listen in on her process of grief and recovery, you will be accompanied by a wise, vulnerable and trustworthy guide. I was deeply impacted by this book, and believe you will be, as well.

Jeff Crosby, author of *The Language of the Soul: Meeting God in the Longings of Our Hearts*

***

It takes courage to be a participant rather than an observer of life. In this riveting account, Julie details her lowest valley through the shadows and the step-by-step process of embracing life while experiencing incredible pain and loss.

Chris Fabry, author and radio host

***

Losing a child is devastating and heartbreaking. The grief is so intense that no words describe the mourning that goes on and on without relief. Breathing is difficult and thinking is nearly impossible. For those whose child took an early journey Home, author Julie Fillinger understands how it feels to say goodbye too soon. In *Courage to Live*, this mother recounts the loss that forever altered her life, her journey through grief to grace, and the life-giving hope found in Jesus Christ.

PeggySue Wells, bestselling author of 40 books including: *The Patent; Homeless for the Holidays;* and *The Ten Best Decisions A Single Mom Can Make*

***

New authors are often encouraged to "write what you know." In *Courage to Live*, author Julie Fillinger writes candidly on a topic no parent wishes to experience - the loss of a child. With both tenderness and full transparency, Julie shares the story of the life and death of her teenage son, Nicholas, and the ways - both painful and slow - she has learned to live with his loss. Though deep grief has been her uninvited companion on the journey, Julie invites others to walk with her through suffering as she offers faith-infused hope and practical help to others navigating this path.

Maggie Wallem Rowe, author of *This Life We Share*

***

As a pastor, when I try to comfort those who have experienced the pain of loss, I wonder if my words ring hollow since I cannot say to them, "I have been there." But Julie Fillinger has. With unflinching honesty and a clear love for Scripture, Julie explores the profound pain of grief and wrestles with faith. If you or someone you love has experienced loss, wondering if God's grace is really sufficient, let Julie be a trusted guide to give you the ***courage to live***.

Dr. Tom Richter, pastor, *First Baptist Church, Cullman, AL*

***

Whether you've suffered the loss of a loved one or desire to comfort others in their grief, Julie Fillinger helps readers direct their hearts to the all sufficient grace of God in Christ. *Courage to Live* is born out of Julie's real life pain in losing her son Nicholas. It's rooted in the sure hope of the Gospel, and it's filled with practical wisdom on how to find true joy in the face of incredible loss.

P. Chase Sears, Senior Pastor at *Tulip Grove Baptist Church, Old Hickory, TN.*

***

Many books have been published about loss and grief, but never have I read a book that so vividly and transparently captures the depth of those emotions as does Julie Fillinger's *Courage to Live*. Any reader dealing with the trauma of loss (especially the unexpected loss of a child) will find here a friend, someone who *truly* understands, and encouragement that gets at the heart of finding **courage to live**. I would recommend this to anyone suffering loss or desiring to help a hurting friend.

Linda K. Taylor, assistant professor, professional writing; author of *Pathway to Publication*

***

Julie Fillinger shares the grief waves that wash over her when she loses her teenage son to a tragic death. She guides the reader through her painful journey by sharing specific strategies and advice that gave her peace, strength, and hope on the other side of the tragedy. A true story that brings light from darkness through her trust in God.

Sandra Baker Baron, author of *Bridging the Mississippi*

Courage
to Live

Learning to Live Again After Loss

julie fillinger

Published by KHARIS PUBLISHING, an imprint of
KHARIS MEDIA LLC.

Copyright © 2024 Julie Fillinger

ISBN-13: 978-1-63746-255-3

ISBN-10: 1-63746-255-7

Library of Congress Control Number: 2024934148

All KHARIS PUBLISHING products are available at
special quantity discounts for bulk purchase for sales
promotions, premiums, fund-raising, and educational
needs. For details, contact:

Kharis Media LLC
Tel: 1-630-909-3405
support@kharispublishing.com
www.kharispublishing.com

AKNOWLEDGEMENTS

Without exception, I must first thank my Heavenly Father who heard my cries, my Lord and Savior, Jesus Christ, who saved a wretch like me, and the Holy Spirit, who would not leave Eric, Drew, and me alone to wallow in a pit of misery.

I am also humbly thankful to many who have made this work possible. Time and space do not permit me to name you all, but here are a few I want to recognize:

A hearty thanks to the entire Kharis Publishing team for taking a risk on me as a new author. I was so drawn to your mission statement, and it was a humble delight when you offered me a contract. With much appreciation for the insights of my content editor, Mary.

To my Facebook family and friends who gave me a safe place to start journaling the thoughts that warred within me and begged to be released: Your encouragement started this journey.

Jeff Crosby, our divinely appointed meeting has been a grace and encouragement from day one. Your kindness and guidance are above and beyond what I could have imagined. I pray our friendship continues.

Pastor Tom and Jackie Richter, as a great picture of the Good Shepherd, God uses your loving leadership to feed and care for my soul. I am the better because of you and eternally grateful for you both.

Heather Williams, my friend, who pushed me to finally launch a website and increase my social media presence, and who is patient with me to come around to what she already knows.

My mother-in-love, Peggy Fillinger, you are my example for living the Courageous Brave with grace every day. It won't be too much longer now.

My mom, Jean Bowling, and sisters, Robin, Tara, and Toni, you love me unconditionally through all of the messiness and have prayed me through every step of this journey.

My beautifully talented and kind son, Drew, you have been asked to live with more courage than any of us. You look out for others as a warrior your brother would be proud of.

My Prayer Warriors, who let me reach out any time day or night and faithfully lift me before our Father's Throne to receive His Grace: Every – Single – Time.

To Eric, the one whom my soul loves,
you are my Hero...still.

CONTENTS

CHAPTER ONE

NICHOLAS'S STORY

D o you have a friend who makes your life better simply by knowing them? They care deeply, often at their own expense, not looking for anything in return. They just want to do good in every area of their life, and they are willing to fight for what is right. They aren't perfect, but their imperfections make them more likeable. This describes my son, Nicholas. I am willing to share him with you and I think you will fall in love.

In October of 1996, we brought home our firstborn son, wrapped in swaddling blankets to ward off the Michigan wind and chill. This was a long expected joy for my husband, Eric, and me. We suffered two miscarriages before I was diagnosed with a thyroid disorder. By then, I was pregnant a third time and was able to deliver our beautiful son, Nicholas, at 36 weeks. I was on bedrest the final four weeks due to pre-term labor. We were definitely expectantly awaiting his arrival.

When we were finally able to bring him home, I never put him down. I just wanted to hold him all the time. My mom told me I was going to spoil him, but I didn't care. When he was about six weeks old, he grew uncharacteristically fussy and squirmy. I had done everything I knew to satisfy him and just didn't know what else to do. A friend who was visiting gently told me he wanted to be put down. In my mind that wasn't an option. Of course he wanted his mom to hold him, but since I had tried everything else, I acquiesced. Much to my surprise and chagrin, as soon as I put him down, he hunkered in and went to sleep. It was hard for me to learn I had been holding on to him too tightly. It wasn't best for either one of us.

Not holding on to him too tightly became a theme that allowed him to grow and pursue hopes and dreams throughout childhood. He was cautious by nature but had enough courage to overcome his fears if he really wanted to try something.

When he was still a toddler, my parents——affectionately called Grandmommy and Granddaddy——bought him a black Little Tykes™ truck and he flew down the hill in the backyard of our Alabama home. We had moved there shortly before his 2nd birthday. His brother, Drew, came along nine months after the move. Nicholas had a stuffed animal he named Drew Bear that he cared for alongside me caring for his baby brother, Drew.

Nicholas wanted to get up early like his dad, but to give me more rest, his dad told him he had to wait until his clock turned 6-0-0. Then he would run down the steps, come into my room to tell me good morning, then get his Pop-tart™ off the counter and milk cup out of the fridge so he could hunker into his chair, and watch an hour of *Franklin and Little Bear©* on Nickelodeon™. This gave me time to rise to the shine of motherhood a little easier as Drew would start stirring at 7:00 AM. Nicholas and I would go in and say, "Good morning baby Drew" and he would smile, laugh, and try to pull our hair. And this is how we would start our day, which mostly consisted of playing with toys.

The boys were both so imaginative, but Nicholas did not play with the toys the way they were designed. He often turned them upside down and sideways, creating some new explorer's station that only he really understood. Grandaddy would say, "Don't you just wonder what is going on in their little minds?"

One time, as we were headed home, a tree had fallen across the road right in front of us. I was afraid it may take hours to be able to get home, but quickly learned that in Alabama this was not a problem. A couple of young fellas came flying around us in their truck, tied a chain around the tree, and hauled it into the ditch. They seemingly came out of nowhere and yet acted like this was an everyday occurrence. They tipped their hats, bid us a good day, and were on their way. Nicholas replayed this adventure over and over tying a rope from his black toy truck to a branch we found in the yard and hauling it off to the creek. His truck was not battery operated; it was powered by his legs and feet. No matter; Nicholas reveled in imitating the heroes he met on that day.

Drew was very cuddly and embraced physical touch. Once Drew was toddling along, he and Nicholas were similar in size. He wanted to spend most of his day tackling Nicholas. I would say, "Nicholas, don't let him tackle you." But Nicholas would just lay there under the weight of his brother, waiting until Drew either got off him or I pulled him off. This process would repeat itself over and over. As they grew, the only time Nicholas was really bothered by his brother was when Drew would "mess with" something Nicholas had created, which was usually made from Legos™. Nicholas locked himself in his room to finish his masterpiece, only to find Drew could get through locked doors.

Having friends over and going to their houses was one of the boys' favorite things to do. We were blessed with very good friends who had children similar ages to ours, so this was something we all enjoyed for many years. New friends came along as the boys' interests in school and extracurriculars changed; being blessed remained.

Things were not always perfect, however. Nicholas didn't get everything he wanted. He was shy and had to overcome some fear to build the friendships he valued. He also had to learn how to deal with boys who picked on him for being small. He was mortified whenever I stepped in, but that was my job.

In middle school, he was on the football team, but didn't start. He didn't make the baseball team, but his best friends at the time did. He played the clarinet in beginner band, but most of his friends were not interested. We spent a lot of weekends at math tournaments where he excelled, but he didn't find everything he was looking for in the wins. He made new friends in track, but wasn't the best on the team, so even this was not quite enough.

We sat together in his room as he pounded the floor and cried he would never be good at anything. I tried to console him, already knowing he was good at so many things, the best of which was the character he displayed in competition and love he had for others. These were growing pains for all of us. Eric has always been better at endurance, so he encouraged Nicholas to stay the course and the Lord would show him the gifts He gave him.

In the summer between middle school and high school, Nicholas was looking for something to fill the void he felt. It seemed to him like diving was going to be the answer. Our local park and recreation department had a good swim and dive program, in which both the boys participated. This provided an outlet through which they enjoyed the friendships that meant so much to them. The high school, capitalizing on this success, was starting a program as well. Nicholas was willing to give up his football aspirations to be on the diving team. Honestly, we were thankful that was settled.

Interestingly, it wasn't settled for long. Right before high school started, Nicholas came home from diving practice and announced he wanted to run in the Midnight Run. This was a well-known 5K sponsored by a local bank in our town. Eric had been an All-American runner in college and ran it every year. There was some prize money, so it boasted some pretty good competition. Even though as amateurs they couldn't claim the prize, many high school and some college cross country runners ran as individuals to gauge how their summer training had come along. Nicholas had shown some aptitude for running at a young age, but he really had not been interested until now. I told him I wasn't sure this was a good idea because he hadn't trained, and I wasn't sure he could finish the race. At this point, he went down to the basement and ran the 5K distance on the treadmill and came back upstairs, not really breathing that hard, and asked again if he could run.

He ran a decent race, and then, at the awards ceremony, we discovered the friend group he was welcomed into as he entered high school. It didn't take long for the upper classmen to bring him under their wings and he bridged the gap between his own freshman class and them. It was nice being a part of the cross country family, where he started enjoying success as he paired his God-given talent with hard work.

It didn't take long to see Nicholas had the heart of a warrior. He was tough, could endure tremendous pain, and was willing to outwork anyone. He never quit. He was fueled by the desire to be the best.

He somewhat idolized a former Olympian and long distance runner, Steve Prefontaine (1951-1975), affectionately known by his fans as Pre. In hindsight, this probably was not a healthy obsession. He watched a movie about Prefontaine over and over. He wrote down Pre quotes all over notebooks. He saw in Pre qualities he identified in himself, especially a willingness to endure more pain than the next guy. Later, we discovered he even used Pre's birthday as a password.

Nicholas had a good sophomore year in cross country, placing in many races. He won his first varsity race in splendid fashion on his favorite course, outkicking a friendly rival to seal victory by .25 seconds. And he was named an All-State runner by placing in the top 15 at the state cross country meet. His track season was also good, medaling at most meets and qualifying for the state meet in three events. Even though he scored points by finishing in the top 8 in the state, he did not medal at the state track meet, so this was a failure in his eyes, which increased his motivation to work harder in the off-season.

There was a lot going on in Nicholas's heart and mind at this point. He loved his team and loved being a part of one. A lot of his friends from the Cullman High School Class of 2013 had just graduated and were moving on to other ventures—college, jobs, the military, etc. Many of his close friends in his Class of 2015 were experiencing their own struggles—some heartaches related to family life, some normal teenage challenges, and some experimenting with things he found concerning. He loved these friends deeply and felt very conflicted.

In addition, his favorite coach had been let go, and he wasn't ready to give the new coach a chance. Even though the new coach exhibited a lot of qualities Nicholas admired, it felt disloyal.

One of the positive constants in his life was his girlfriend, Jessi. They were sweet together, treating one another with respect and deference. They supported each other's interests and were a constant source of encouragement to one another. You didn't feel awkward around them but enjoyed the young love they had for one another. You could tell it was rare and special. She was one of his best friends, and they laughed together more than anything. She didn't get upset when they ordered off the value menu or when we needed his brother, Drew, to tag along.

The summer between his sophomore and junior year, Nicholas trained hard. He was aided by some growth and was very strong to start his junior year. With so many changes, he felt like he could control this, but he was obsessed with being the best. He researched times and techniques and worked on improving in every aspect of his running.

This is when he informed us he needed to do altitude training. He had to. It was a must for his improvement. We don't live at altitude, so we weren't sure how to accomplish this. We asked another gifted runner about using an altitude tent, but she didn't find it helpful and said it made her sick. So, we thought he had let this go.

About this time, he went on a discipleship weekend with Cullman First Baptist Church and came home more humble and more respectful. He seemed renewed in his devotion to Jesus Christ as his Lord and Savior. He made a commitment to join their chapel choir and planned to go on choir tour, even though he would sacrifice parts of 12 days of training the summer between his junior and senior year. He said this was more important because it was a way to share the Gospel.

His junior season began just about as well as it could. Nicholas won the first cross country meet of the season, beating out several other gifted and highly touted runners in the area. He placed 2nd in meet #2, and then medaled at a large meet that hosted quality running programs from several states. Meet #4, he placed 2nd again but broke the school record by 6 seconds. After the awards ceremony, he re-ran the course with his distance watch as a cool down to make sure it was the proper length, which it was. Cross country meets in high school are 5K and his watch tripped to 3.1 miles as he crossed the finish line. I tried to encourage him by telling him he could just break that record again.

Only, neither one of us knew that was to be his last race.

I have thought about every day of the following week over and over. What could we have done differently? What signs did we miss? How did this happen? Some of the days are a blur, but Thursday is crystal clear.

When he came home from practice, he was twirling his lunch bag around. I was sitting on the couch, ready to greet him and talk about his day. I was in between jobs and relished these opportunities. On this day, I asked him if he would pick up Drew so I could go talk to a friend. He readily agreed because he knew this was important. I got home just in time to meet the family at the team meal. At the meal, Nicholas talked with one of his best friends and teammates, and they made plans to talk more later. This was encouraging to Nicholas, given the team dynamic at the time. Only "later" never happened.

Nicholas and Drew drove home ahead of Eric and me. And as soon as we walked in the door, Nicholas quickly turned off the computer, as if hiding something, and rolled his desk chair over to ask me if I tried to get one of the members kicked off the team. Apparently, this was some of the discussion at the team meal. I told him I didn't want anyone kicked off the team, but that I had spoken with their coach because I wanted every member on the team to act right and to get back to treating one another like a family. Nicholas wanted the same thing, but was embarrassed that his mother spoke to the coach.

Nicholas then started to head downstairs to start his bedtime ritual. He did his usual pull-ups and sit-ups, but Thursdays were especially important for sleep to be ready to race on Saturday morning. I stopped him and said, "Hey Nicholas." When he peered his head around the corner, I said, "I love you." To which he replied, "I love you too, Mom." Then he headed downstairs.

Drew was already downstairs, so Eric and I sat on the couch and talked for a while before checking on them.

What happened next is the shocking trauma that is forever etched in my brain. It plays over and over in slow motion, as if on a Ferris wheel that won't stop and won't let me get off.

While Eric and I were talking, Drew suddenly ran upstairs and was crying that something was wrong with Nicholas. We ran downstairs to find him hanging from the shower rod. I immediately picked him up by his legs and Eric easily and quickly removed his head from the belt that was loosely looped around the shower rod and his neck. He was unconscious and not breathing and we couldn't feel a pulse. Because of our professions, we were both able to use our training in CPR. We started but couldn't get a good airway because he had vomited. Eric wiped out his mouth with a towel and tried to give a couple of breaths.

We couldn't see his chest rise and looked for an obstruction. *Was this actually happening?*

I started chest compressions and Eric called 91.[1] EMS responded quickly and took over. We were in shock. The police also responded and started investigating the scene. Eric called Drew's Uncle Wayne to come get him. It seemed like a long time before the rescue team brought Nicholas out to the ambulance. We were to follow them to the ER. By this time, a crowd of friends and neighbors had appeared outside. We told them where we were headed.

When EMS arrived at the ER, they took Nicholas into a trauma room and a team there was performing rescue efforts to save him as we waited outside the door. I just kept pleading over and over, "Please, Lord, please save him, please save him, Lord. We will give You all the glory. We know You can save him. Please, Lord."

After some time, which is a blur, the ER physician took us into a separate room and told us things did not look good. I pleaded with him to keep trying. I remember asking him what the protocol was for young, healthy 16-year-old boys. He said even if he were to survive, he would be very sick. His heart was beating erratically, and he had been deprived of oxygen for too long. I refused to accept this. "No, no, no, no!" I cried this over and over. Because of my pleading, he said they could keep trying a little longer. And he let us into the room.

What happened next feels like an out of body experience, like I was watching it unfold from the corner of the room. It sounds like a bizarre ghost story. The moment we were led into the trauma room, I sensed the Holy Spirit bringing the Bible story of King Hezekiah[1] to my mind. He had pleaded with God to give him more time and God relented, and granted him 15 more years, but it wasn't the same. I remember thinking at the time I studied this passage it would have been better if King Hezekiah had gone on to Heaven than to live his remaining 15 years. They were not good years and not representative of his life prior. Of all the passages I have studied in the Bible, the Holy Spirit brought this one to mind and strongly impressed it upon me. It washed over me as I had the eerie sense that I had to let Nicholas go.

Time seemed to have stopped for these few seconds. Then it became clear that even if God saved him, it wouldn't be the same, and it would be better for him to go on to be with his Heavenly Father. The Holy Spirit was urging me to say in my heart, as my Lord had said, "Not my will, but Yours be done, Father."[2] I looked up at the team that was continuing to work, and I said, "It's okay, I know he's gone." Then I saw that everyone, including Eric, had already realized this. I saw their painful expressions as they were hoping I would come to the same conclusion. I can't remember who all was in that room as I looked from person to person, but I will never forget the absolute empathy of that ER physician. He was in anguish as he called the time of death, and they all stopped. I came up and cupped Nicholas's face and kissed him. Eric did the same.

We live in a small town and word travels fast. By this time, Wayne had arrived with Drew, and Eric's dad was also there. His parents had moved to Cullman two years before. His mom has multiple sclerosis and remained at home, faithfully praying. My sister, Robin, worked out of town at this time but was on the way. Robin lived with us for several years when the boys were young, and they loved her dearly. In addition, our friends, as well as students, parents, and administrators and faculty from school had gathered in the waiting room. They were crying, praying, and hugging. They were all escorted to a larger room so we could address them.

We told them we didn't understand why this had happened, but we thanked them all for being there for us and told them how much Nicholas loved them. At the time, Eric and I thought Nicholas had taken his own life, even though it didn't make sense. No one in the room would accept that. I was somewhat taken aback by how his friends completely rejected this idea. Nicholas had made plans that he would have completed. Jessi's family was there with her and said there is no way he would not have said goodbye to her. She said he texted her earlier in the evening, but he had not read her reply. This is when we realized we may have a timeline from Nicholas's phone. She explained that he had his read receipts turned on so they would know if each other read their text. It was important to us to get his phone.

As it turns out, the police had his phone. They picked it up off the bathroom floor during their investigation, but couldn't get into it without the password. Jessi had told us it was Pre's birthday. They looked through it for just a little while, but then gave it to us. They said they did not believe his death to be a suicide, but were ruling out whether Nicholas may have been involved in some kind of oxygen-depriving arousal game. We had never heard of this, and the authorities eventually ruled this out as well.

When we left the ER, we had more questions than answers. Nothing made sense. We searched his phone and saw that he had been texting and then suddenly stopped. We saw the last text he sent and that he had not read the last response from the guy he was texting. They were talking about whose mom had talked to the coach. Nicholas pretty much knew it was me, but the other guy said it could have been his mom too. This is the response Nicholas never read. The time from this first unread text until we got to him and started CPR was 40 minutes. Jessi's text came in between, and he never read it either.

The next morning, Jessi's dad came over with his computer. He had been up all night trying to make sense of it all. He told us that they had watched a special broadcast that summer on swimmers who could hold their breath under water for insane amounts of time and then still function in an oxygen-deprived state. He said he remembered thinking at the time that Nicholas seemed very interested in this. He was the first to come up with the theory that Nicholas was trying to mimic altitude training by depriving himself of oxygen, but still forcing his brain to function while performing some perfunctory skill, such as texting.

We didn't know what to think and desperately wanted to know the truth, but this did make the most sense. We found one of the problems was he never told a single person he was doing this. The police took our computer, and nothing came up in a precursory search. It would have been easy for Nicholas to erase the history, and since there didn't appear to be any foul play, they didn't search any further. The police ruled the death an accident, and that is what is on the death certificate.

We wanted to be sure, and continued to look for other clues. We recalled previous conversations and found a book we had given Nicholas for his 16th birthday on training success. It talks about the importance of altitude training and discusses the chemistry behind it. Nicholas had been studying his chemistry book with more fervor than normal. We thought he was trying to be a better student.

We went on to research how one could imitate altitude training. There seemed to be a couple of favorite options among athletes, especially runners. One was an altitude mask that you wear, and it deprives you of oxygen while training. We found no evidence that Nicholas had purchased one of these. The other is taking a belt and using it to put pressure on your carotid arteries, just until you are depriving yourself of oxygen, and continuing to force yourself to function so you can teach your brain how to perform in low oxygen situations, like in a race. We found that runners know not to do this by themselves because they could pass out, and they need a buddy to be able to remove the belt. They usually use their bedpost to loop the belt through. Nicholas did not have a bedpost; the shower rod was the only thing in the house sturdy enough to hold him while he stood on the edge of the bathtub.

This was the most ridiculously stupid thing we had ever read. And what evidence is there that it works? It certainly is not worth the great risk of losing your life. We could not believe our smart child would engage in this behavior. And yet...it was possible. Running success was one of the most important things in his life and he wanted to prove he could break the school record again. Could he have done this, passed out, and then accidentally hung himself when his head dropped forward?

Even though we continued to wrestle with whether this was the truth, it did seem to be the most plausible. Just typing these asinine words makes my head spin and my stomach ache at how ridiculous this is.

The next few days are a blur. Funeral arrangements, caskets, burial plots—parents should not have to plan these things for their child. A friend met us at the funeral home, which was helpful as we were in shock and needed the encouragement to make seemingly impossible decisions.

The whole community showed up with money, gift cards, food, paper goods, and supplies to last months. The school came with banners students had made and cards they had signed. Nicholas loved people and wanted to be around them, but he could be shy. Many spoke of his kindness and his smile as well as his standing up for what is right and his faith. Letters poured in from other runners who spoke of his good sportsmanship as he shook their hand on the line, then raced against them as fiercely as he could.

The cross country meet went on as scheduled on Saturday. We were able to get on the bus and address the team as they were heading out and tell them what we suspected. We encouraged them to forgive any past wrongs and love each other as that would honor Nicholas's memory best. We did not go to the meet, but hundreds showed up and cheered as the athletes ran in his honor. They made a large circle and one of his teammates prayed in the middle.

Family and friends started coming in from all over the country: my mom, whom the boys called Grandmommy; my two other sisters, Tara and Toni; Eric's brother, Rod, and sister, Dorinda, and all their spouses and children, as well as aunts, uncles, and cousins and their families. Our local friends welcomed them all into their homes or paid for them to stay in hotels. Their hospitality was incredible. One of the local owners of the Hampton Inn™ had a son who was in Nicholas's class and was a friend. They put up many people at no charge. A local favorite restaurant, Johnny's

BBQ, fed the entire family of around 56 people before his visitation (which lasted hours as people were in line wrapped around the building). Nicholas was well-known, well-liked, and well-respected. Flowers and plants took up two whole rooms at the funeral home, many from cross country teams from all around the state. The shocking nature of it all brought people out who couldn't believe it or make sense of it. Neither could we.

A couple of hours before the funeral, we went to say goodbye and close the casket. It was necessary and gave us some privacy with just the family, but I hated this part. It forced some reality on me that I wasn't ready for. I remember being worried he couldn't breathe.

It was important to us for the funeral to honor Nicholas's memory but also to glorify God. Cullman First Baptist Church allowed us to have the funeral there as about 1200 attended that Sunday afternoon. A friend played the violin, his favorite instrument. Another friend led us in a favorite hymn. The chapel choir, which Nicholas and Drew had joined recently, sang *Mercy Seat*©. Wayne preached on qualities that characterized Nicholas's life: Invest, Persevere, Finish, Win. Even though Nicholas's life ended tragically, he had lived a good life with good character and that is what people would remember about him. Pops,

Eric's dad, preached passionately about judgment and mercy and getting your life right before it is too late. Overall, I think we accomplished the goal.

Nicholas's friends carried out the casket. Many walked the short distance to the burial. We read verses and prayed and left. I knew from burying my father that I did not want to watch the casket being lowered into the ground. The cross country team and some close friends stayed and helped shovel dirt on the casket as it was being lowered.

We went back and had a meal with family and close friends at the church. Then when it ended, it was time to go home. No one wanted to face that reality. We had been living in a rental house, which now felt like a place of death, and the porch was lined with plants from the funeral home. We were in the process of closing on land to build our long-awaited dream home, but it felt more like a nightmare. We were emotionally homeless for months. Our builder was a friend, and he got us in to our new home as quickly as possible, which was good, because there were times I thought I may blow-up what felt like the death house.

We moved Drew and all things pertinent up from the basement so we didn't have to go down there, but the washer and dryer were there. I bought us more underwear, and we went downstairs as little as possible. Every so often, I would make myself go down there to face little bits of reality. It took a while to build up the strength to go in the bathroom, and when I did, there were Nicholas's clothes as he had left them. I pulled them to myself and held them for a long time as if I could will him back into existence. I often asked God to bring Nicholas back from the dead, and I promised to give Him all the glory. Even though He said no, I kept asking.

Somehow, by God's grace, with the help of friends, and thousands of decisions later, Blake built us a home. When it was time to move in, we had not touched Nicholas's stuff. It had been seven months, and everything was how he left it: his bed, his books, TV, memories, and everything of material importance to him, which wasn't much. Eric and friends mostly took care of packing up the basement, so I didn't have to. When they pulled his basket of dirty clothes off the moving truck, I lost it. I remember wanting to escape, I could barely breathe. Our new home was beautiful, but how could we move in without one of our children?

The walkout basement was designed to be an apartment for Nicholas and Drew together, who were both teenagers; then later in life they could bring their families and have some room to be comfortable. Only now, Drew was going to be down there by himself. We encouraged him to stay in a bedroom upstairs, which he did for a short time, and then Eric let him get a puppy.

I am not one to act like pets are people, and it really irks me for someone to act like they lost a child when their dog dies. But we did get our westie Jack when my father died and named him after my dad. And we got our cavapoo Toby for Drew after Nicholas died, and his name means God is good. And they both have been a comfort.

∞ ∞ ∞

The rest of this book is about surviving this great loss. I will share with you the raw and honest pain I endured, struggles with anger at God for not saving Nicholas, and realizations that were not always welcome. Some days the only reason I survived is because the alternative was not to live the life God called me to. While that is a choice I have wrestled with on more than one occasion, I cannot bear to merely exist. As I waited on God for what felt like a very long time, He picked me up out of the pit, set my feet on solid ground, and put a song of hope in my heart.

My desire is to inspire you to believe, by God's grace, you can endure more than you ever thought possible, because you have courage to learn how to live again after loss. So when you get to the end of your life, people will see you as a living breathing testimony of God's faithfulness and place their trust in Him. God has forever been faithful. His children have full assurance to expect their inheritance is secure, waiting for them in Heaven to be revealed at the right time. This is our Blessed Hope.

CHAPTER TWO

THE COURAGE TO LIVE IN PAIN

Intense grieving did not begin right away. I wasn't being phony, but shock and the Holy Spirit gave me an appearance of dealing seemingly well with the loss in the immediate aftermath. I remember thinking God would be faithful to get us through this. And He has been, but when I was initially determined to rely on Him, I had no idea what He would be asking us to endure. I had never experienced anything like this. It was about to become worse than I could imagine.

I have been hesitant to describe the severity of the pain of grieving a cherished loved one. While the description may resonate with some, I fear it may alienate others. I do not want to discourage anyone from missing the hope that grace gives. I concluded, however, that it may do more help than harm. This chapter is intense. My hope is, if you hang in there, you will realize you are stronger than you think.

The graphic nature of raw and honest misery could be rated M for Mature, except who ever reaches a level of maturity at which they are ready to experience the pain of grief? When Nicholas died, my heart was stabbed over and over with a dagger that brutally twisted until I passed out from the physical pain, only to be awakened and realize this was not a dream. It wasn't even a nightmare. It was a horrifying scream that came from a dark place where hot fire burned and never went out; you know, the kind that's so red its edges are purple. It never lost its intensity or ability to destroy. The scream echoed in my ears until I felt like I was going mad. The stabbing pain was a welcome comfort compared to the scream. How could I dull the screeching magnitude of its volume? What could I do to numb the pain? At best, I could drown it out for brief moments, while it continued behind a closed door, but the scream beckoned to be heard. Relentless in its pursuit, it refused to stay shut out. I felt like I was in hell physically, mentally, and spiritually, like God was far from me and had left me alone in separation. I did not even have the strength or wherewithal to ask, "Why God?" I cried out until there were no more tears to cry, leaving me in heaving sobs of confusion and bewilderment, begging for relief.

This went on for the better part of the first year. Merely existing between moments of terror is basically what I did. Just performing the perfunctory daily activities was how I got by. The pain of grief was so intense at times, I did not think I could bear it. It was a miserable existence. And then it would eventually break, and some relief would come; the times of terror would lessen. Finally, sometime in the second to third year, I wavered between merely existing to wanting to live again. I either needed to die or live. And if I was going to choose to live, then I needed to really live, not just exist.

If grief was linear, I would have been able to rejoice in relief. I had made it through, yet I soon discovered grief was not something I could get through to the other side. I could not finish one phase and move on to the next, never to revisit the previous depths of hellish anguish. It has been more like overlapping cycles that loop back on themselves, and eventually progress forward. The cycles can repeat, not necessarily every phase or in the same order, but with a similar familiarity.

During this time I realized that seemingly contradictory emotions can coexist. It was possible for my heart to be broken but still live fruitfully and productively; to be in constant pain, but still have something to give others.

I had been working for Eric part time until the year before, and I was ready to get back to what I wanted to do in my nursing career. I had applied for a couple of jobs that seemed promising. When Nicholas died, I didn't even go to the interviews.

We were also building our dream home as I said. We had been working toward this goal for twenty-three years. We had the plans, the land, and the builder. I honestly do not know how we managed to make the thousands of decisions necessary to build a house. We closed on the land just a few days after the funeral. Our builder was great to work with. He had the right amount of patience, compassion, and drive to push us to do what we needed to. Then on move-in day, one of us wasn't there.

Since I wasn't working outside the home, it was probably good to have the house project to work on. I would like to be able to tell you Jesus was my motivation to keep on, that I wanted to do God's will and seek Him first in all things. The truth is it was Drew. Eric and I could have possibly talked each other into taking a sedative and falling asleep with the car running and the garage door closed if it were not for Drew. I know that sounds dark and maybe surprising to some, but thoughts like these occurred more than once. Sometimes my thoughts were more passive, like not wearing my seatbelt and not caring if I died in a car accident. It seemed one of us was feeling a little stronger when the other was weak. "What about Drew?" we would say. "You're right," was the reply. The first year, I was the weaker one, mostly because Eric did not get to stay home and grieve. He owns a business and returned to work the following week after Nicholas's funeral.

A freshman in high school, Drew was only 14 when his brother died. His high school career was punctuated by this tragedy. He could not get away from it. None of us could, and it seemed disrespectful to Nicholas's memory to try. So, on the days we did not want to push on, Drew filled our hearts and minds. We had to keep going for him. He was still here and he had a beautiful life of his own to look forward to.

Living for Drew and not for God has placed an unintended burden on Drew. God has been dealing with me on this. He calls anything I put before Him idolatry.[1] It was not my intention to live for Drew, but especially the first year, he was my motivation. Even though He is faithful in His loving kindness and patience towards us, God does not want us to live for anyone but Him. He is the only One worthy of this kind of adoration.[2]

Looking back, living for my children was a struggle long before Nicholas died. As I said earlier, we suffered two miscarriages before Nicholas. By the time we were blessed with his arrival, longing that turned to expectant joy soon left me feeling guarded. It's not that I was overprotective, but the previous losses helped me realize how quickly things could change. I wanted to be the best mother I could; it was my number one job. I would not take anything for granted. I was determined to enjoy my children thoroughly and was thankful to be able to stay at home with them. When it came time for them to go to school, I loved being a part of their success there as well.

When Nicholas was in elementary school, there was an author spotlight in the library. Nicholas took to being a young author. He wrote twenty-eight stories in third and fourth grade, and the librarian compiled them into the *Nicholas Fillinger Collection*. She had kept it and passed it on to us after Nicholas died. One of the stories was entitled, *Definitions to the Things that Make you Better*. In it, he defined concepts such as respect, self-control, honesty, courtesy, mercy, fairness, being nice, and courage. His definition of courage stands out not only because he lived courageously, but also because it has now become necessary to my survival. He said courage does not mean you are not afraid; it is being afraid and doing it anyway. How many times was he afraid, but he pressed on to do some hard thing, to do something he didn't want to do, but did anyway? Why didn't I help him see as a child that he did not have to be so brave all the time, or at least he didn't have to be brave alone?

Merriam-Webster defines courage as "the mental or moral strength to venture, persevere, and withstand danger, fear, or difficulty".[3] If courage is when you have fear, anxiety, or sorrow that could keep you from doing something, but then you go ahead and do it anyway, what gives you the strength to do it despite the wrestling emotions? And why does it seem like some people have more courage than others? I had good examples of courage growing up. There were people in my life who overcame difficulties to do hard things, but I know plenty of people who had no such examples and exhibited amazing courage in spite of their circumstances.

There seems to be a sense of drive and purpose embedded into the actual living out of this concept. It sounds like Christian cliché, but my strength ultimately came from the Lord when I felt like quitting. He used good examples to encourage me and give me a picture of what it looks like. When I would have let go, He held on to me. God was faithful to instill the drive and purpose to live while still in pain. I had courage to live even though I was in pain, but I was not alone. I did not have to do it by myself because God was with me. The times I felt He was not with me would become fewer and less intense. At the time, it felt like waiting on the Lord would be my new life. It felt crushing to go seemingly long periods without hearing from Him. I could not see it, but He was using the waiting to build endurance, which I would need as part of this courage to live in pain.

A year and a half after Nicholas died, I went back to work as a psychiatric nurse in a community mental health clinic. I worked with clients who had also suffered greatly and in ways I could not have imagined. Many struggled with abusing substances to numb the pain, and I honestly understood the temptation to do this once I had suffered greatly myself. Ministering to them gave me such a different perspective. I did not share my whole story with very many clients, but I think I was a believable broken person and this seemed to resonate with my client base. Even though my job mainly dealt with medication, if they opened the door, I did take the opportunity to share some aspects of my faith as the hope of my existence. I never forced my faith, but if they asked and were receptive and it seemed it would be beneficial to their healing, I wanted them to have that hope too—not beating them over the head, but just sharing a single truth that seemed appropriate in the moment. Then letting the Holy Spirit take it from there.

Usually an act of kindness, such as a gentle squeeze of their hand or a pat on the back, was enough to start to gain their trust. They did not often experience kindness from others, so the warmth of the expression was healing. It felt good to do something, however small, to help others who were suffering in ways that seemed unimaginable. And because I knew what suffering felt like, I knew I could do it.

As time has dared to march on, joy and sorrow coexist in my heart. I cry easily and feel deeply. I still focus too much on anniversaries, and I cannot seem to stop this. The date is a trigger for me. I get angry when I see the numbers on the clock or someone's athletic jersey, like they are taunting me. I continue to relive the horrific trauma in the weeks leading up to death day. The beginning of the school year ushers a call from the dark places of grief which intensifies as the day draws nigh. My heart hopes for a different outcome "this time" and is cut to shreds when the different outcome does not happen. My head knows this is foolish, but my heart still struggles to accept it. I catch myself thinking that it did not really happen, that Nicholas is on a trip and he will be coming back. I feel sucker punched in the gut when my head says, *foolish girl, the sooner you come to grips with it the better*. And round and round it goes.

Now, it is not as bad as it has been. I have learned to practice better coping skills, replacing lies with truth about who God is at the core. I do not feel brave, but I ask God to give me the courage to live each day He gives me. I ask for courage, and He gives it. Sorrow and sadness are there, but not always at the forefront, not taking up all the space in my heart and mind. Because of the Gospel, joy can exist alongside sorrow and even take center stage. They have become intertwined, woven into my life now. Joy co-existing with sorrow makes it a little easier to endure the hard things like living from day to day and helping others do the same along the way.

As I continue to reflect on the definition of courage by a young Nicholas, I cannot help but consider that fear is a real part of courage. You're afraid, but you do it anyway. Fear and grief are not that different, especially in their paralyzing nature and struggle to move forward. You're grieving but you do it anyway. What is the "it" that you're doing? It is living. As you keep on keeping on in your cries to the Lord, He will be faithful to hear you, lift you out of the pit of despair, and place your feet on solid ground.[4] Then you will realize He has been with you all along. The Holy Spirit living inside of you will testify to your spirit that His presence is with you.[5] You are not living alone.[6] The courage to live in pain means you don't want to go on, but you do it anyway, trusting God will make sense of it in His time and use it for His Glory and someone else's good.[7] Along the way, God in His faithfulness and by His Spirit will continue to cultivate the fruit of joy alongside the pain.[8]

CHAPTER THREE

WHEN DOES IT GET BETTER?

T here have been milestones in my grief journey. I have no doubt this will continue. The first year has been the hardest—all the firsts without a part of my heart. I could only grasp a little of the realization at a time. My head knew the truth, but my heart would not allow me to accept it. My heart felt like it was betraying me by letting some truth in. Feeling panicked and wanting to scream in agony like a wild beast, I tried not to let it in. *How could I accept this horrific realization that I am going to live the rest of my days without my beloved firstborn? This cannot be happening.* I wanted it to be a bad dream that I would wake up from, and it would all be over, but that was not the case.

As I said, I would pretend Nicholas went on a trip and he was coming back. Only he didn't. He missed the rest of cross country, track, choir tour, the rest of his junior and senior years, prom, graduation, and all of college. And the pain was sharpened with each dream that was not realized. We had so many plans. He would have had academic and athletic scholarships to college. He wanted to train for the Olympics. He wanted to marry his high school sweetheart. *Why didn't we get to see these things happen?*

Shortly after Nicholas died, I walked into a department store that specializes in home décor, among other things. While shopping, I saw many decorative crosses that lined the aisle. I don't even like fancy and colorful crosses as they seem to lack authenticity. When I happened upon the robin's egg blue colored cross with "It is Well with my Soul" written across the top, I was not prepared for the flood of emotions that filled my heart and mind. I wanted to smash that cross right there in the aisle of the department store while screaming, *It is not well with my soul, it's not by a long shot!* I was able to keep my composure as I quickly exited, but it took me some time to contemplate why I'd had such an emotional response to seeing these words painted on a cross. As a Christian, shouldn't it be well with my soul?

I believe God in His perfect design created us with a body, soul, and spirit. Most people understand and agree our bodies are the material, physical part of us. However, there is disagreement amongst theologians as to whether the soul and spirit are combined or separate entities used to describe the immaterial part of a person. Do we have a soul/spirit or a soul and a spirit? These views are classified by the terms dichotomous (body and soul/spirit) and trichotomous (body and soul and spirit).[1] I have spent a good amount of time researching the differences. While I can argue an intelligent point of view from Scripture in favor of a dichotomous view that references theologians I turn to for guidance in handling God's Word, I would not be completely convinced of that which I was arguing. Are there things God did not intend us to completely understand? While it is true some things will continue to be a mystery this side of Heaven, God does want us to understand that which He has revealed in His Word by His Spirit.[2]

When I turned to the Bible study fundamentals of observation and word study, I discovered soul and spirit are closely related but distinct. In the *Complete Word Study Dictionary of The New Testament*, Zodhiates says soul and spirit are closely related because they are both immaterial and both contrast with the body, but there is a distinction between them. He goes on to say that they cannot mean the same thing because they are mentioned together in 1 Thessalonians 5:23, spirit and soul and body, and the same distinction is brought out in Hebrews 4:12.[3] Furthermore, I cannot get past the trichotomous creation of man in Genesis 2:7: God formed man physically from dust, He breathed into his nostrils the breath (spirit) of life, and man became a living soul.

Whether or not we agree that soul and spirit are distinct, perhaps we can agree our body, soul, and spirit are unified and interactive.[3] When something happens to one, the other two parts are affected. When grieving, there is an emotional response to sorrow. Your soul cries, is easily agitated, and feels void of love. There is also a physical response. Your body physically feels the weight of sorrow. You are so tired and drained of energy. You may experience changes in weight and appearance. The spiritual response to grief affects changes in communication with good and evil spirits. It is hard to sense the Holy Spirit's presence connecting and leading your spirit. He is still there but seems drowned out by the sorrow and anger. This makes you vulnerable to attacks from evil, and why you feel like you are in a dark pit.[4] Prayer lifts you out of the pit and reconnects your spirit to the Holy Spirit Who has been there all along.[5]

Not all that we learn from Scripture in regard to the inner man is met with as much controversy, such as being made in the image of God. Like God, we have an immaterial part of us that houses our mind, emotion, and will.[6] It is what makes each of us unique as a person. The spirit is the immaterial part of us the Holy Spirit testifies to and where He leads and guides.[7] If you are God's child, the Holy Spirit dwells in you to help you discern between good and evil.[8] Evil can oppress you but not possess you when the Holy Spirit is taking up residence.[9]

With this understanding, the reason I responded adversely to "It is Well with my Soul" was because I am in the process of being sanctified, becoming more and more like Christ until He returns.[10] At that time, I will be made the completely finished person God intended me to be without the presence of sin.[11] There is a part of me that is well because God deemed it so at the point of my salvation. When the Heavenly Father sees me, He already sees the work of Christ through the sealing of His Spirit.[12] Even when the darkest of hours tries to tell me otherwise, it does not change the Truth of my salvation. God saved me and how I feel does not reverse the action that took place at the point of my conversion. Sin no longer has the same power over me, but its presence is not yet completely removed. So, my emotions fluctuate and my head and heart disconnect. It is sometimes well, but sometimes not. I will not be completely free of this struggle until I am free from the presence of sin when I die or Christ returns.

Perhaps you join the thousands of Christians who love the hymn, *It is Well with my Soul©*. Maybe the words have directed your worship as you praise the Lord. Many people told me the story behind the lyrics after Nicholas died. When I researched it for myself, there were many accounts to sift through to find the truth of the hymn writer's biography. What I discovered was Horatio Spafford was an attorney who lived successfully in Chicago with his wife and daughters. The Chicago fire of 1871 destroyed his home and real estate investments. He booked passage on the *SS Ville du Havre* to get away on a vacation and join Dwight L. Moody's evangelistic campaign in Paris. He sent his wife and four daughters on with plans to join them as soon as he could after unexpected business dealings would allow. He did not know that was the last time he would see his daughters.

All four of them drowned when the British sea vessel, *Loch Earn,* crashed into the *SS Ville du Havre* while crossing the Atlantic Ocean. His wife was still alive when a rescue boat arrived and brought her to Paris where she sent a telegram which read, *"Saved Alone...what shall I do?"* Spafford boarded another ship to join her as soon as he could. He penned the beloved hymn as a poem a few weeks later as the ship passed over the spot where his daughters perished. It would be a few years before Phillip Bliss, a composer who travelled with D. L. Moody, would set this hymn to music.[13]

It seemed it should comfort me to know someone else suffered such a tragic loss and still praised God, but something about loudly proclaiming, "It is well with my soul" bothered me. I could say it is well with my God or it is well with my spirit. Sometimes I could say it is well with my soul, but not always. I researched the life of the hymn writer further to discover it was not always well with his soul either. Spafford's life was punctuated by one tragedy after another, including the death of his son that was born years later, only to die from scarlet fever at the age of five. He and his wife did have two more daughters, but not before he left the Presbyterian church where he was an elder and started a gathering for his followers at his home in Chicago.

Amidst calls from creditors demanding he pay his debts, Spafford moved to Jerusalem and started The American Colony, where his followers joined him. By this point he denied the reality of eternal hell and preached Universalism, a belief that God will save everyone even without repentance of sin. He felt the return of Christ was imminent and that Christ would start His reign with Spafford and his followers, so there was no need to pay debts in Jerusalem either. After a few years there, he was said to be hallucinating and delusional, most likely from malaria to which he eventually succumbed. His wife continued his work as a prophetess in Jerusalem after his death.[14]

I do not rejoice in this man's losses or tragic circumstances. Considering he penned the hymn very shortly after the deaths of his daughters, he did not know the depths of grief to which he would later plummet. I do not doubt he meant what he was writing at the time he was writing it. It later became clear it was not well with his soul.

When my soul is struggling, it's easy for me to be angry at God. After all, He could have done something to save Nicholas and He didn't. Nicholas was a great kid. Why didn't God want to keep him on this Earth? It's not because God needed another angel; I cannot pray to Nicholas, and he doesn't come to visit me as a different form of God's creation. The truth is, God numbered his days and the number He gave him when He formed him in my womb is the number he received.[15] On this earth, that is. When Nicholas's work on this Earth was complete, His Heavenly Father brought him Home to Heaven.[16]

Is Heaven better than anything here on this Earth? God tells us this life is a vapor.[17] It does not feel like a vapor. It feels long and laborious. It did not always feel this way. I grew up in a loving home with two imperfect parents trying to do the best they could to love, provide for, and protect me. I did not realize most people do not grow up like this. It was not until I went to college that I heard other people's stories of hurt and loss. God started using this to make me more empathetic, but my story remained mostly happy well into adulthood.

I met Eric in college. We got married, struggled financially in the early days, moved around with school and jobs, and had two kids. Life was not perfect as we struggled through disagreements mostly brought on by selfishness, but it was pretty good, better than I deserved or recognized at the time.

Then my father died shortly after my 36th birthday. The week after his death, I wrote a short story entitled, *God's Grace and Mercy in the Life of a Daughter*. I told of how merciful God was to take my father's life quickly in an auto accident. He was suffering from peripheral artery disease and would most likely be bed ridden, which he would have hated. At the time I wrote it, I meant every word, but I did not know the depths to which I would shortly plummet. His death shook me to the core, and I intensely grieved the loss for five years. It was one of the worst things I had experienced up to that point. I was a daddy's girl, and he was a #girldad before it was cool. He represented God's love and protection and provision. I felt lost. I missed him so much. This was just a precursor of what was to come. As great as this loss was, it did not compare to the misery that awaited.

God did, however, start to use it to teach me about thinking eternally. I had already been pondering and studying what Heaven was like, but this search intensified when Nicholas joined my daddy in Heaven. What were the two of them doing? Was it better than athletic accolades, prom, graduation, college scholarships, marriage, having his own children? My conclusion is an emphatic YES!

If we lived here on Earth with the reality of what awaits us in Heaven, we would pray for Christ's return every day.[18] There is nothing here that compares. God created everything here to give us a picture of the glory that awaits.[19] There is nothing better than being in His presence. Nicholas's and my daddy's souls and spirits are both present with the Lord.[20] It's a glorious comfort and hope. When Christ returns, the dead in Christ receive their eternal bodies first.[21] They keep their personalities and giftedness and use them perfectly for God's glory and for all of eternity.

It's not harps and clouds. It's like the Garden of Eden,[22] only there's no way to mess it up with sin.[23] We have purpose and work we enjoy, good conversations over good food and drink. Beautiful gardens and music. Dancing. Competitions for the joy of it.

If I believe that Heaven is so much more glorious than anything this Earth has to offer, I will slowly start to believe it was good for God to take my loved one there with Him. He didn't make us for this life, He made us for the next one.[24] This is so hard for me to fathom, but God will be faithful to fix the eyes of His children on what matters. When does it get better? It gets better when I start thinking eternally. When does it get better? It gets better when I fix my eyes on Jesus and the blessed hope to come, for only then can I endure the present suffering.[25]

CHAPTER FOUR

IS GOD'S GRACE REALLY SUFFICIENT?

D o I really believe in the sufficiency of God's grace or not? I thought I did, truly. Then the awful worst happened and it was tested, repeatedly.

What does God's sufficient grace really mean? God is shedding favor on me? It doesn't feel like favor. And this is supposed to be enough? Because it is not. I did everything right. I did not deserve this. I loved God. I obeyed Him. I served Him. I raised my children to do the same. I was the best wife, mother, nurse, daughter, sister, and friend I knew how to be. I gave God all the credit. I knew I was nothing without Him. My faith was strong—until it wasn't. Maybe I subconsciously thought God owed me something in exchange.

My beautiful firstborn child was taken away. I cried out to my Lord and my God, begging Him to let me keep him, begging Him for favor. I had not asked for much but I asked for this: *Please Lord*

God, do not take my child. Please Father in Heaven, please give him back to me. Isn't the world better with him in it? Please do this and we will proclaim your Glory to the ends of the Earth. Everyone will know this could only be You. And I believe with every fiber of my being that You can do this. All power in Heaven and Earth are in Your hands.[1]

Do you know what He said? No. He said No. It wasn't because I didn't exhibit enough faith. He said No because it was His Will to do so.[2] My world was crushed. The pain was greater than anything I could ever imagine. A dark hole consumed me, and I did not want to climb out. I felt completely wasted and weak.

But over time and some other things the Holy Spirit was doing to put my broken heart back together again, I began to realize I was in the greatest spiritual battle I had ever faced. And I was losing. Had my faith just been this fragile thing with no substance?[3] I had been tested before and God's grace had pulled me through.[4] This was different. I was not sure I wanted to pull through.

In this battle, one of the questions I have been laboring over is whether one of my sins caused Nicholas's death. Did God take Nicholas's life because I sinned? It is only recently that I even gave voice to this struggle. In other words, is there a 1:1 correlation between sin and death?

Do you remember the sin of King David with Bathsheba?[5] It is one of the biggies in the Bible. By the time the warrior David became king, he had fought many battles. God was faithful to deliver him, but he was understandably tired. He stayed home instead of going out to yet another battle with his brave warriors. They loved war, David was ready for peace. However, staying home did not produce the tranquility he longed for, and soon he became restless. He went out on his roof and saw a beautiful woman bathing. He should have turned away, but instead he lingered, and this turned to lust. He was the king. Why shouldn't he have what he desired? He sent for Bathsheba and committed adultery. She became pregnant and David murdered her husband to cover it up. David then brought Bathsheba into the palace as one of his wives. It's not until the prophet Nathan confronted him that David was repentant. When confronted with sin, David saw his wickedness. He saw sin as egregious as God saw it. He asked for mercy and God spared his life and the life of Bathsheba, but God took the life of the baby.[6]

David's sins of adultery and murder were so egregious because he was supposed to represent God's character to God's enemies. Instead, he scorned the LORD by openly breaking His commandments. David's child died as judgment for his sin. In the New Testament, Jesus holds us to the higher standard of what's in our heart. If you lust, you commit adultery, and the heart of anger toward your brother is the same heart of a murderer.[7] Am I no better than David in my sin?

Why would God take the life of the baby? The baby was innocent. Yet God said he died because of David's sin. We see how the death of David's child was part of God's judgment of David's sin, but how is it also merciful not only to David, but also to the child? Bathsheba's husband Uriah was one of David's mighty warriors.[8] The child from Bathsheba and David's adulterous union would have been looked on unfavorably at a time in history when the penalty for adultery was death.[9] God took the baby to Himself to live with Him for eternity.

In order to see this as a mercy, I must accept that Heaven is much greater than anything here on Earth. Without that wholehearted realization, I would think the child missed out on growing up in the palace with a mom and dad who loved him. I would think his life on Earth was better than what Heaven had to offer. In reality, what he missed out on was a difficult existence here on Earth, and in its place he lived in Glory. Nothing could be better. David said he would join him in eternity.[10] In this world David would have trials and tribulations but looking at His life through the lens of the Gospel would show him and me, that Jesus Christ has overcome the world.[11] It's not this life that matters, it's the next one.[12] Does this not also show the grace and mercy of God amidst His judgment of sin?

My husband and I said early on that we were not going to blame each other. I still cannot help but wonder if I brought about Nicholas's death with my sin. So, I am back to asking if God took David's child because of his sin, did my sin cause my son to die?

I could look at the life of Job as another example.[13] In comparing David to Job, there is obvious sin in the life of David, as opposed to poor Job, whom everyone accused of doing wrong. Job never even knew the God of the universe was permitting Satan to approach Him as He was holding up Job as a standard of faith and righteousness.

Job's children were taken because a greater purpose was at play. God knew Job would remain righteous even if everything was taken away.[14] I have never felt as righteous as Job. I identify more with David's wretchedness.

Maybe I can find some clarity In the New Testament. Jesus said the blind man was not blind because of sin but that God's Glory would be manifested in his healing.[15] Considering this, I asked my pastor about my struggle and how I should view sin in regard to the New Covenant.[16] This is what he had to say:

> "It is not that the New Covenant dismisses justice. Death was and is the penalty. But the death we deserve was borne by Another. The Old Testament drives us straight to Calvary. You might say there is still very much a 1:1 correlation!
>
> 1 -lost world who rejects Yahweh and rebels against His covenant love leads DIRECTLY to the death of the
>
> 1 -(only begotten) Son."[17]

Did my sin cause my child to die? I won't be completely assured of the answer this side of Heaven. There is comfort in knowing that identifying with David is not all bad. Yes, we are both wretches, but our hearts are redeemable. How else could God call David a man after His own heart?[18]

Unless the LORD God of the universe performs heart surgery, I would be stuck in the misery of my sin, but He doesn't leave me there. He removes my heart of stone and replaces it with a heart of flesh.[19] This transplant occurs while I am still dead in my sin. I'm a helpless, hopeless sinning enemy of God when He calls me out of the dark and into the light.[20] And He puts His Spirit in me to testify truth to my spirit.[21] So now when I sin—like my brother David—the sin grieves me. David wrote beautiful songs of repentance as he was grieved over his sin.[22] He saw sin how God did. May I always see my sin as God sees it. For only then will He say, like He did of His child David, I am a woman after His own heart. I can let go of the guilt of sin and all its possible consequences that God's only begotten Son already paid for.[23] It will most likely come up again, but God will be faithful to help me in the struggle to come to the same conclusion. His grace is sufficient.

It seems now I could let the question of the sufficiency of God's grace go, but new struggles would arise. If God's grace was sufficient to save and keep my soul and spirit for all eternity, and my child's soul and spirit for all of eternity, was it sufficient to make me whole again?[24] The thing about spiritual battles is, you must be willing to put on your armor and fight.[25] It is not going to feel like a fair fight. Satan and his minions fight dirty. I had to discover that if I was going to win this battle. The battle was not really mine; the battle was the Lord's, and so was the victory.[26] There is more power in one puff of His breath than Satan's entire army and arsenal of evil combined.[27] I just had to yield to Him.

Why exactly is it so hard to yield? Why does fighting a spiritual battle feel like it should be my fight when He has told me He will fight for me?

The willingness to engage in the battle is all about submitting to the will of the One who made me, gave His Son to save me, and is willing to keep me forever.[28] It feels so backward from my natural understanding. Because it is. God-things defy human logic. I keep trying to exact human wisdom and crumble when it doesn't work. I continue to fail to understand His power is made perfect in my weakness; when I am weak, then I am made strong.[29] People tell me I am the strongest person they know. I tell them it is His strength at work in me. I am nothing. He is everything. He saved me and He will keep me.[30]

How did I learn to lean on His grace during the hardest trial of my life? It started before the worst happened. I had mentors who poured into me long before I was tested. My mom was a prayer warrior and showed me how to be kind, loving, and forgiving because God had forgiven me.[31] Growing up, I went to church camp every summer I could, and even worked there one year. I was nine when God opened my eyes and showed me my need for a Savior at the church camp bonfire.

I had a Sunday school teacher in high school who mentored me and thought more of me than I deserved. It was not until I was in college that I wanted to learn how to study the Bible. I was at a revival conference and felt convicted that I had not been living the life God called me to. When I confessed this, God put a hunger in my heart to know Him more, but I didn't know how. So, I asked God to show me. It took some time. I started by reading five verses at a time. Every day I would add five more verses and ask the Holy Spirit to teach me what it all meant. Slowly, He started to help me understand. This was also about the time I met the man who would become my husband. Eric knew a lot more than I did about the Bible and he was patient in teaching me.

Getting a good study Bible was very helpful also. I wasn't always consistent; this took years to develop and more mentors teaching me, but God was faithful to stay after me and His Spirit kept nudging me. Little by little, when I responded in obedience, He grew my faith.

Strangely, as I grew in my faith, there was a temptation to take credit for it. Which makes no sense. I will discuss this more in chapter 9, but one of the premises of salvation is to be poor in spirit, to realize there is nothing I can do to earn my salvation.[32] I bring nothing. It is all God doing the work.[33] The key to staying humble is to never get over what God did for me by giving His Son to die in my place so I could live.

I knew this, but needed to be reminded and needed to be thankful. I deserved death in hell, and He gave me Eternal Life. When Jesus Christ conquered the grave, He took away the sting of death and proclaimed victory forever.[34] The work He accomplished on the cross when His Son paid for my sins was enough. So, once again the conclusion is God's grace is sufficient to save me and my son and to keep us for eternity.

What does He ask of me? He only asks me to keep looking up[35] and stay connected to Him.[36] Just as He was faithful to pursue me all those years ago, He continues His persistent pursuit. He is the Faithful One, not me.[37] When I am prone to forget, He will be faithful to remind me His grace is also sufficient to heal me as I continue to learn to live victoriously with the coexistence of joy and sorrow until He returns.

CHAPTER FIVE

RECYCLED COMFORT

I first heard this phrase from my pastor while sitting in church. I do not remember everything he said, but the impact of the message was one of those "Aha!" moments. This is what the Holy Spirit had been trying to tell me. You know when the Holy Spirit is testifying truth to your spirit and your head is bobbing up and down, like the pastor can't get the teaching out quickly enough. An audible, "Hmmmm," breaks out into, "Yes, Lord," and, "Amen." This was one of those moments.

"Recycled comfort" comes from 2 Corinthians 1:3-7:

Praise to the God of All Comfort

3 Blessed be the God and Father of our Lord Jesus Christ, the Father of mercies and God of all comfort,

4 who comforts us in all our affliction, so that we may be able to comfort those who are in

any affliction, with the comfort with which we ourselves are comforted by God.

[5] For as we share abundantly in Christ's sufferings, so through Christ we share abundantly in comfort too.

[6] If we are afflicted, it is for your comfort and salvation; and if we are comforted, it is for your comfort, which you experience when you patiently endure the same sufferings that we suffer.

[7] Our hope for you is unshaken, for we know that as you share in our sufferings, you will also share in our comfort.

The trauma we endure can be used to comfort someone else when they are going through something similar. The comfort we receive from the Holy Spirit when enduring unimaginable suffering and loss is recycled and given freely to the next person God brings your way. Then, in due time, that person will take the comfort they received and give it to the next person God brings their way. And on and on it goes.

It's as if the genealogy of comfort were to be traced back to its spiritual roots, we would see the faces of those heroes that came before in the "Faith Hall of Fame";[1] those brave but ordinary people, soldiers in God's Army, whose battles we have heard about for generations and are witnesses of the same. The comfort they received in their time of need is the same comfort we receive now. It is comfort that has endured. This comfort has waged war and come through victoriously time and again because it comes with Spirit Power.

The same power that raised Jesus Christ from the dead is at work in us[2] in the form of the Holy Spirit testifying the truth to our spirit that this pain, this suffering, is not wasted.[3] God's purpose may not be readily evident, but our suffering will be used. The Recycled Comfort that suffering brings to the next brave soul will be inhaled as the life-giving intoxicant that could only come from the holy breath of a Savior who has endured the same.[4]

You can be sympathetic and even empathetic, even if you have not endured the same trauma. But there is something connective between two souls that suffered a similar but shocking predetermined destiny. You can see it in their eyes, the window to their soul. You hear it in their voice, the greater degree of understanding. You can feel it in their touch when you collapse in their arms and receive a gentle but firm reassurance that you can make it. They don't feel the need to say much and are comfortable in what normally would be awkward silence.

God gave me encouragement early in my grief journey by crossing our paths with other parents who suffered child loss. It was obvious that He prepared our hearts at His right time. One such time was when we walked into a Mexican restaurant and saw a couple we knew, Tori and Jim. Their son had died a few years prior. They were sitting closely on the same side of the booth as if they liked each other. They invited us to join them. Their faces expressed warmth, but not so much that it made us break down in tears. They did not feel the need to ask us how we were doing. There was an unspoken understanding that they knew the answer. It was not awkward at all. They spoke easily with hopeful words that were not forced. They squeezed our hands, acknowledging what we were feeling and facing was pure misery. The experience instilled real courage in our hearts and backbones. They were a living testament of survival. So maybe we, too, would survive. We did not make plans to get together, but God brought us together on a few more occasions. Each time was a similar uplifting experience. The Holy Spirit had knitted our hearts together in like-minded kinship.

God has given me the opportunity and honor to walk alongside others as well. Even though each story is as unique as the individual who passed on, there are similarities in the suffering.

Whenever God uses me to minister to another mom, I thank Him for Tori and her willingness to minister to me when I desperately needed it. She gave me two books that were especially helpful. *Surviving the Loss of a Child: Support for Grieving Parents,* by Elizabeth Brown helped me find words to describe the pain of grief through the heart of a like-minded mother.[5] *One Minute After You Die,* by Edwin Lutzer gave me the assurance I longed for from God's Word that my son was in the presence of Jesus and there was no better place for him to be.[6] We received many other books as well, some helpful, others not as much. What made the books Tori gave me stand out was because they were works God used to minister to her, and since the Holy Spirit was leading her to minister to me, it was likely God would use these books to minister to me as well.

It has been important for me not to force these relationships. Sometimes people introduce me to someone who has been through something similar. They want to do something to help ease their pain but do not know what to do. Their intent is very good, but if it isn't naturally part of God's plan, it doesn't work out. But if I "happen" to come across the right person God wants me to minister to, the encounter is so uplifting it can only be described as miraculous. God will bring those He wants me to reach out to in His time.[7]

I am prayerful about who to reach out to and I gauge by their response if the Holy Spirit is nudging me to follow up with more. If God places someone on my heart, I act on it. I pray for them, and then I wait for more leading. Sometimes it's a prayer, a text, a lunch meeting, taking a meal or book to them, a hug, a card, or a combination of these. I am not good at waiting; I'm given to action. But I know the wait is an important part, so I do it with the help of the Holy Spirit.[8] Being in tune to the leading of the Holy Spirit is crucial in discerning what and how much to do. It takes practice to know if that was the Spirit nudging or just my own feelings. I don't always get it right.[9] But God's tender loving kindness is new each morning; great is His faithfulness.[10]

When the time is right and I reach out while my own heart is broken, something spiritually bigger than me takes place. I get to be an instrument in the hands of an Almighty God. I feel Him doing the work through me. He lets me be a part of the process—a healing agent in the hands of the Sovereign Ruler of the Universe. It's very powerful, and my own broken heart is mended in the process.[11] I have become addicted to this process, this being used by God in a miraculous way that gives real comfort and courage to the hurting. All loss touches me more deeply now. I am keenly aware of the suffering the mourner is about to endure. If the loss is a child, my empathy radar is especially elevated. I feel sick. My chest and stomach physically ache with grief. I know what is about to happen, and it is miserable. They need courage to make it through the coming days.

There have been several moms who have suffered child loss that the Lord has been gracious to use me to encourage. Misty and Kelly are two of them and have given me permission to share their stories.

Misty's Story

Misty's son died after a difficult pregnancy and harrowing delivery. It seemed as though God was going to perform a miracle in his young life. Many were praying and praising the Lord. We knew only God could heal him and we gave Him all the Glory. Then, after a short time, he suddenly died. So many confusing moments and waves of emotion during the pregnancy and in the aftermath. Why give the hope he would live and then cruelly take it away? Misty was devastated. What could I do to ease her pain while I was angry God did not do what we wanted?

When Nicholas died, I knew I would do it all over again, even if I knew ahead of time what was going to happen. I would take as many days and moments as God would give, even knowing the pain and suffering I would endure when his short

81

life ended. The Lord patiently reminded me of this when I was praying about how to comfort Misty in her time of grief. All I said at first was, "This is awful," and, "I am so sorry." I kept checking on her and continually prayed for her. In time, I gained her trust enough that she was willing to talk about her pain and sorrow. I was a believable broken person and that helped break down any walls that threatened to let me enter. In time, she wanted to celebrate her son's life. His life mattered and will be remembered. I joined her in the celebration. Our friendship continues and we have expanded the relationship to other aspects of life's joys and sorrows, which include others in our families as well.

Kelly's Story

Kelly has a different story, but no less traumatic. When her son was introduced to the evils of this world, he battled and overcame, just to battle over and over again. He grew so weary of the war that waged inside, he eventually stopped fighting and took his own life. It was tragic. Since I am not completely sure Nicholas did not take his own life, I well-remembered the struggle with guilt that plagued me, which was mostly born out of my own pride and believing lies. It really didn't matter how he died, as much as he was gone and I couldn't bring him back, no matter how much I tried to will him back into existence. What was of comfort to me was the hope of seeing Nicholas again. Now God was giving me the grace to minister to another mom with a broken heart.

Kelly felt certain her son had made a profession of faith, so she also did not grieve as those who have no hope.[12] We have spent time crying with one another and encouraging each other not to believe lies. We cry out in our pain, knowing the other understands and will be faithful to lift us to God's Throne of Grace.[13] I am a little further along in my grief journey, so I can give some perspective that God has *forever* been faithful.

I think our friendship is a testimony to others in our groups of friends of how God put us together for such a time as this. Our faith has been tested and it has been strengthened. Even though we continue to struggle, we keep concluding God's faithfulness will be available to help us overcome the suffering that pales in comparison to the Glory that awaits.[14] And we praise God.

My prayer is that God will continue to use my story to minister to hurting people as He leads and that it will instill in them the courage to press on. In time, may they recycle the comfort they received to minister to other hurting souls. And on and on it goes until Christ's Glorious Return.

The following have become my life verses:

"I waited patiently for the LORD; He inclined to me and heard my cry.

He drew me up from the pit of destruction, out of the miry bog, and set my feet upon a rock, making my steps secure.

He put a new song in my mouth, a song of praise to our God. Many will see and fear and put their trust in the LORD" (Psalm 40:1-3).

CHAPTER SIX

AN UNWELCOME REALIZATION

I t was around year five, when it hit me that God wanted to use our faith story more than Nicholas's. This realization was unwelcome. I had grown accustomed to telling Nicholas's story and I wanted him to be remembered. As time went on, it wasn't as though people forgot him, but the world dared to move on without him. We were still here as living, breathing testimonies of loved ones who had survived a terrible loss. Telling Nicholas's story was important, but over time, what seemed to have more significance was how God had been faithful to us and would continue to carry us along the journey.

It has taken me a long time to be able to begin to even try to put this into words. I feel like I am somehow forsaking Nicholas's memory if moving forward, I am open to God using my story more than his, yet this is how I feel the Lord leading.

One question I had to answer is why is it so important to tell Nicholas's story? Sure, I can see how it can be used for God's glory to share the Gospel and raise awareness for an orphanage we support. And it is understandable that a mother would want to keep a child's memory alive through a scholarship in his name. We are even willing to ask tougher questions about unsafe training practices to keep what happened to him from happening to other competitive athletes.

If I look deeper though, I see that I think God made a mistake in taking him. I tell myself it is because Nicholas wanted to use his success to bring glory to God. Why wouldn't God want to keep a beautiful child like him on this Earth to be used to advance His Kingdom? I can even see where I struggle with not trusting God to know what is best for my children, holding on to them with a closed fist instead of an open palm, recognizing they are really His.[1] I have confessed my sin of making my children an idol.[2]

But the deep-down real reason

it was so important to tell Nicholas's story,

instead of telling how the tragedy

has affected me,

is I felt guilty for surviving.

How could I survive this great loss? And not just survive but have times of laughter and happiness. If grief is the price of love, how am I able to get out of bed? Does this mean I do not love my son? These are the questions that plagued me as I kept putting off completing this book.

I have known the truth in my head, that God wants me to share with whoever has ears to hear that He did this amazing work in my heart. All the glory belongs to Him to allow joy and sorrow to coexist until Christ returns.[3] My hope rests in the saving work of His Son that makes a way for me to look forward to Eternal Life.[4] I have shared these truths little by little over time.

Then my heart would disconnect from my head at times when I needed it to stay engaged. It would lie to me and tell me if I survive and even thrive after such a great loss, I didn't really love at all.

To think I didn't love my son with every fiber of my being may be more painful than losing him.

It has taken all these years to say that; to recognize the hold that lie had on me and to finally release it to my loving Father who is faithful and can be trusted with my deepest hurts.[5]

So, what now? I still struggle, but since I have been able to see it for the lie it is, I can try to move forward. Surviving the loss does not mean I did not love my son. Now I can ask God how He wants to use me surviving this great loss for His Glory.[6]

As stated in the previous chapter, He brings people my way to whom He wants me to minister. As I follow His lead, the lies lose their power. I can truly use the suffering for God's glory in these other ways too.

The orphanage I referred to earlier in this chapter is called Not Forgotten. It is family-centered orphan care located in Iquitos, Peru. You can check it out at www.notforgotten.org. The first Christmas after Nicholas died, Eric and I were desperate to do something in his memory. Our friend, Destin, told us about Not Forgotten. This orphanage is unlike any we have heard of as it seeks to introduce vulnerable children to the hope of Jesus Christ by providing holistic, individualized care in a healthy family environment intended to give them hope and break the cycle of abandonment. We have been able to go to the orphanage twice for a week each time. We are thankful for the opportunity to support the children, parents, staff, and missionaries.

We also started the Nicholas Fillinger Foundation. The Nicholas Fillinger Memorial Run is the sole fundraiser for the foundation. It is a 5K run on Nicholas's favorite trail, St Bernard Trails located in Cullman, AL. The support from sponsors has been incredible over the years. These are people and businesses who believe in what the foundation is doing, want to encourage us, loved Nicholas, and want to do something in his memory. The Run is held in the middle of July because this is a natural break for cross country runners to check on their summer training. It averages about 160 participants of varying levels of competitiveness, which is pretty good for our small town. Nicholas loved running as part of a team, so teams are a favorite aspect of this Run as well, providing a unique element to a local 5K. So many family members and friends from our church and community come out as volunteers, that the participants can't help but comment on their service.

Right before awards are handed out, some part of Nicholas's story is shared in the greater context of the Gospel, with the hope that someone will hear and place their trust in Christ. The whole spirit of the day is one of love and encouragement from a competitive endeavor that seeks to glorify God by using the memory of one of His children to advance His Kingdom.

In addition to supporting Not Forgotten, the foundation gives a modest scholarship to a graduating senior who will be attending college. The Nicholas Fillinger Memorial Scholarship Award looks to capture the spirit we saw in Nicholas. Ideally, this is a high achiever academically and athletically, but most importantly has good character, competes with passion, loves their teammates, and looks out for the underdog. Nicholas was a passionate and fierce competitor, but he was not perfect. His flaws showed his humanity and that he was someone with whom others could identify. I fear his death lifted him to a status God did not intend. We pray the recipients feel honored but not pressured. May they be encouraged to seek God's will and goodness in their life's purpose. For only in Him will they find peace and meaning.

Finally, the Foundation seeks to research safe training practices in an effort to educate other athletes of potential dangers to prevent what happened to Nicholas from happening to anyone else. Eric has been able to speak with some local coaches and presented to some teams early on, but this is as far as it has gone. We pray for God to open doors as He wills. May we be willing to courageously walk through them as He brings opportunity.

It has been healing for us to use Nicholas's memory to bring Glory to God and advance His Kingdom.[7] However, Nicholas would not want us to use his name. As much as he was passionate about winning, he did not seek the spotlight. As grieving parents, we wanted to keep his memory alive and so we've used his name in these endeavors, but I have been wondering if it puts more focus on Nicholas's glory than God's.

Perhaps it would be more appropriate to change the name of the foundation but keep the run and scholarship the same. God continues to be gracious as He shows me how to serve Him. In my grief, it can be a struggle to keep God the primary focus and not Nicholas.

However, my chief desire is to glorify my Lord. I get up every morning and ask God what He has for me that day—every day, just God and me. And in the quiet of the morning, He teaches me how to courageously live this life after tragic loss.[8] And He asks me to be willing to be used by Him as an example of what He has done.[9] Here it is written in this book to be used for His Glory however He sees fit. My prayer remains that others will see and put their trust in Him.

CHAPTER SEVEN

PRACTICAL STEPS

No one wants to suffer. We go through elaborate means to try and get out of feeling pain, which we discussed in an earlier chapter, but it is unavoidable. Up until this chapter, I have been telling my story. You may not be able to relate completely, but if you have suffered loss of any kind, or know someone who has, then there will be some commonalities. This chapter is intended to give you some practical things you can do to get out of the pit and stay out.

What is the pit? The pit is the place grief takes you where you feel the most despair. In addition to generalized depression and anxiety, there is an overwhelming and paralyzing sense that you are being overcome, that God is allowing you to be sifted by Satan.[1] You feel like you are falling into a black hole, and you do not know when you will hit the bottom. Panic grips you as you wrestle with realizations you are not ready to deal with. When you finally do hit what you think is the bottom of the pit, you have no idea how to get out.[2] And you are not sure if you want to try because the effort is too great. God seems very far from you.[3] You are open to more attacks from the enemy, tempted to believe his lies.[4] You wallow in the contemplation of dark thoughts, your insides are screaming in agony, and relief is all-consuming.[5]

The pit is not a good place to hang out. When you first sense you are starting to fall in, or even before, here are some action steps to consider:

Step 1. Call on your Prayer Warriors.

It is essential to ask at least five people to be your Prayer Warriors (PWs). These are your people. You can call on them at any time night or day and have confidence they will lift you before our Heavenly Father's Throne of Grace.[6] You will know who to ask because they will be the ones who keep telling you they are praying for you and asking you what they can do. You can tell they mean it. If you do not know, then ask the Holy Spirit to reveal this to you, and then ask them. Ask them. Yes, this includes the introverts. I have a few more than five, but that thought is too great for the introverts who may be able to come up with three. Regardless of the number, where two or three are gathered, God will be faithful to show up.[7]

This is necessary when you feel yourself falling in the pit. You may feel like you don't want to bother them. Do it anyway. They have already agreed ahead of time and have identified that they want to do this. Do not let pride get in the way.

What happens when you call on your Prayer Warriors?

The very act of asking requires humility which God delights in as it shows your utter dependency on His power.[8] It engages others in the battle, solidifying you are not alone. One of Satan's tactics is to isolate—he wants you to feel alone. You're not.[9] Their obedience in lifting you up before the Father cannot be underestimated. It is the first link in the chain. Then Jesus, the Intercessor, personally takes the request before the Father. Out of His great love, He once again stands in the gap. As if His death on the cross was not enough, He continues to be the bridge and our access to the Holy Father.[10] The Father hears and will not deny His Son anything requested in accordance with His Will.[11] The power is unleashed! He commands us to come boldly and promises to give grace in time of need and that is exactly what happens. He has been utterly faithful to this promise. Every. Single. Time.

His grace still amazes me. Every time I have called on my PWs in time of need, God has been faithful not only to spiritually and emotionally lift me up, but also physically as well. I can physically feel the lifting.[12] Try and prove me wrong. Just when I think, *it won't happen this time, I'm not going to get relief,* I call out and relief comes. I then think, *why, oh why, did I wait so long to cry out?*

What if you wait until you are at the bottom of the pit to cry out for help?

You're struggling in the darkness and you see no way out. You finally decide to utter some semblance of a cry. Keep on crying out. Just keep on. And then when you have just the tiniest gumption to call on your PWs, do it. One at a time. Do it. It may take longer to feel relief because you have spent extra time in the dark, but it will come. And then next time, do not wait so long.

Step 2. Cultivate a Heart of Gratitude.

Nothing transforms your broken heart like being thankful. Ann VosKamp has already written on this subject. Go today and order the updated 2021 book, *One Thousand Gifts*.[13] It is life changing. Reading it the first time took me about nine months to get through. I was so grief stricken I had a tough time remembering what I was reading. Then God used this work to encourage me at a time I was surrounded by darkness. I did not want to keep living after Nicholas died. Honestly, being there for Drew was my only motivation, but I was tired of living half dead, too. When I picked up this book, the truths she pointed to from God's Word spoke to me in miraculous ways.

How could being thankful so drastically change my outlook on my circumstances? You need to read the book to be fully engaged, but to summarize, when we choose to be thankful, we open our hearts to let light in. The light exposes the broken pieces, which is painful but necessary. Then the bands of thankfulness wrap our broken heart and hold it together until the pieces have time to mend and grow stronger.

You will not automatically cultivate a thankful heart. It will not come naturally. You must make yourself count things for which you are thankful. Day after day. Counting and recounting. Then you put them all together into the messy masterpiece of your cultivated heart of gratitude.[14] Many days you do not feel like being thankful; you would much rather complain and wallow. No one would blame you. Be thankful anyway. If you cannot think of something to be thankful for, consider Eternal Life.

Reflect on what God did in sacrificing His One and Only Son to pay the price for your sin. He is not asking you to endure anything He did not endure Himself.[15] Nicholas knew Jesus Christ as His Lord and Savior, so I have hope to see him again. I cling to the Blessed Hope of Eternal Life.[16]

Step 3. Show Love.

How is it possible to reach out to others all the while your own broken heart is shattered in a million pieces? You take that heart that has been bound together with the cords of thankfulness, and while you are still basking in its miraculous favor, you act in love. You do something you would not normally do. You show some act of loving-kindness. These acts of love fill in the broken pieces like salve, thus continuing to cultivate the heart of gratitude while the action is taking place. Living this way is absolutely contrary to our nature, and impossible in man's strength.

But God... But God.

These two powerful words are the antithesis to man's way of thinking. There are man's fruitless self-centered ways and then there's God. And all the objections fall flat in the reality of what God can do. When you live with courage every day, looking for ways to show love to others while your own heart is in desperate need, you show a picture of what God's love can do.[17] You could have the opportunity to make an eternal impact. The significance of this does not disappoint.[18] There is a reason for the pain. There's hope in the healing.

Those three steps are the ways I fight to live another day. The alternative is not to live the life

God called me to. And even though that is a choice I have wrestled with on more than one occasion, I cannot bear to merely exist. I want to be able to say, like my brother Paul, "For to me to live is Christ, and to die is gain." (Philippians 1:21). I am not afraid to die and go to Heaven to live out my eternal days, but I am choosing to stay and live on this Earth for as long as God has Kingdom Work for me to do here. I know when God's time for me has come, He will take me to be with Jesus.[19] And I will also get to see Nicholas.

The What Elses

In addition to those steps, doing some other healthy things are helpful. These are the What Elses. As in what else can I do to learn to live again after loss? These include a healthy diet, exercise, sleep, good music, and Bible study.

Even though I struggle to do them, I know I should eat better and exercise. When I do them consistently, I feel better. Honestly, they can seem too great a hill to conquer when you are trying just to live to the next hour. It is helpful if one of your prayer warriors can double up in accountability with diet and exercise. My struggle here continues but lessens as I continue in the fight.

In full disclosure, in the first nine years after Nicholas died, I gained 30 pounds. I like to blame grief and menopause, but pizza and cheeseburgers on the weekends may have played a role as well. In all seriousness, I have just recently had a little boost in energy and have come up with a reasonable walking, weights, and diet plan. I have lost 27 pounds. Not many seem to notice, but I keep at it.

Sleep is essential. I struggle every single night to fall asleep, but it has gotten better. I have tried various combinations of over the counter medication under my physician's guidance. So far, I am satisfied enough that I have not pursued other sleep aids. I also find listening to restful music on a timer as I fall asleep helps settle my thoughts. I knew when I laid my head on the pillow, my thoughts were going to be consumed with grief. I would dread it. I started asking my prayer warriors to pray for me to be able to fall asleep, and I disciplined myself to turn the music on.

It certainly helps to be disciplined to make myself go to bed at a regular time. If I know I don't have to get up early the next day, I can easily stay up too late binge-watching or reading. Night-time Julie is not a friend to morning Julie. Morning Julie has cursed night-time Julie on many occasions. I do not love being disciplined. Night-time Julie says, *why can't I just stay up and do what I want?* Then I would crash and wonder how this happened. Morning Julie was there waiting with a smirk. When I became more disciplined in my sleep, I developed a much healthier pattern for being disciplined in other areas, like walking and dieting.

Another essential is filling your mind with truth about who God is. Satan wants you to believe lies. He is the father of lies and he wants to rip your life apart so he can accuse you before God's Throne. He knows he won't win in the end, but wouldn't it be a victory to take you down, at least make your life ineffective for God's Kingdom?[20]

When you feel so weak and unable to even formulate a good defense, struggling to remember all those things you know to be true about who God is, *music* gets through. Music. I know I just talked about music helping quiet my thoughts so I could fall asleep, but it is also very helpful in letting truth in. God designed and authored music to resonate in our souls. It transcends the mutterings of our lips and thoughts of incoherency in times of deep sorrow. Listen to good music that reminds and teaches you the truth about God's character. This will tear down the destructive lies that threaten to wallpaper your mind and replace those lies with a healthy knowledge of Who God is.[21] Music should be on every day.

I love God's Word. When I am not in His Word, I feel far away. Until you can start or get back to making good Bible study a consistent part of your routine, buy a children's bible story book. My pastor's wife recommended *The Jesus Storybook Bible: Every Story Whispers His Name*, by Sally Lloyd-Jones.[22] Maybe you grew up with these stories in Sunday school and they will be a good reminder of who God is. Even if you are reading these for the first time, God will use the truths to help you in the fight against Satan's lies. If you absolutely cannot focus on a single word, go back to just music for a time. Then try again asking God, by His Spirit, to help guide you. He will be faithful.

Most likely, people will be giving you books or telling you what you should read. It is important to read truth; truth does not contradict itself. Scripture interprets Scripture. If you are God's child, the Holy Spirit lives in you and will guide you, if you ask.[23]

If you are not sure you are a child of God, please read chapter 9 and make certain right now. There is no time to waste.

While the three practical steps are the main considerations, the "what elses" will be good goals to strive for to aid in your survival and healing. I hope you have found them helpful. I am committed to praying for every person God uses this book to reach. Even if I do not know you by name, God does. I can bring even the un-named before His Throne of Grace for healing and courage as they learn to live after loss.

CHAPTER EIGHT

DO THIS, NOT THAT

When someone we care about is hurting, we want to do something or say something to ease their pain. If we are being honest, in part, we want to ease our own discomfort as well. Seeing people in pain is uncomfortable for everyone. We all just want it to go away. We are a comfort-driven culture and there is no place for suffering.

The bravest souls are willing to endure personal discomfort so they may provide some measure of relief to the hurting. If you are reading this chapter, then perhaps you are one of those brave souls—or at least you want to be. Either way, I hope you find this useful. I compiled these lists from what I found helpful and not helpful when others tried to comfort me while I was in pain.

For practical purposes, let's look at what to do and say and NOT to do and say to comfort anyone who is suffering loss.

Do This

1. Practice what to say.

The most appropriate thing to say is (are you ready for this?) .... "I am so sorry". Meaning, I feel great sorrow over the pain you are having to endure. It makes me hurt too. So, I am sorry. I hate this tragedy. It is awful. You did nothing to deserve it. It stinks. These are all appropriate as well, but can be summed up in a heartfelt, "I am so sorry". It sounds too simple, but when said in earnest, it really was the most helpful.

2. Check your face.

Depending on how close you are to the hurting person you want to minister to, your facial expression will say a lot. If you are very close and showing anguish—this is appropriate, and you can try to comfort one another. If you are not the person's best friend, but you want to reach out, your facial expression should show concern, not despair. Even if the hurting person is suffering the greatest of tragedies, keep your face from telling them how great a tragedy this really is. They are not ready for that. If you show up with a meal and are sobbing or looking pained, the hurting person will be thinking, *wow, this must be really bad.* They will instinctively want to get you out as quickly as possible because they can only handle little bits of reality and your face is telling them they must handle it ALL right then.

3. Ask yourself how uncomfortable you are willing to be for this person.

You will endure more discomfort for someone you love. If you are not that close, do not feel like you must do this. If you are willing and you sense the hurting person is open to you staying, just sit in uncomfortable silence and hold their hand. For as long as they will let you, just sit there, doing nothing, being uncomfortable together. Then, when you have shown you are not afraid of the pain, and even though it is uncomfortable you will endure it with them and for them, you can ask, "What can I and may I do for you?" They may tell you something that would be of help.

4. Allow them to feel as normal as possible in public.

They have used all the energy they have to get out of bed and get dressed and halfway presentable. When they finally make it out, give them space to just be there to get their tasks done. Do not acknowledge them with an overly warm expression. This is NOT the time to say, "I am so sorry". They are trying to hold it together; being overly sympathetic will not let them do that. Saying "hello and I am praying for you" is appropriate. Then let it go and let them move on to the task at hand.

5. Hospitality in moderation is good.

It is okay to bring meals and flowers and send cards and gift cards to let them know they are loved and prayed for, but consider spreading it out over the first weeks and months after the loss when they really need it. Getting too much food or too many flowers and plants all at once is overwhelming. The person feels guilty for having to put it in the trash. They do not feel like eating, but need some nourishment, so moderation is most helpful. It makes a difference if there are children to be fed. Also consider how big the family is. To be honest, we lost track of some of our gift cards and then found them years later and enjoyed them then.

6. Consider writing out prayers and mailing them.

My cousin wrote out her prayers for me three days a week and mailed them the whole first year. It was incredible. Many times, she was praying God's Word. This may not be comfortable for everyone, but we are close like sisters, so it was welcomed. To say I am praying for you is good, but writing out your prayer will be even more encouraging.

7. Say their name.

Some people are afraid to say the dearly departed one's name for fear of bringing more hurt to their loved ones. This is not possible. They want to hear their name. They want them to be remembered. Share stories and pictures and reminisce. Having good memories is a blessing and a comfort to remember.

8. Consult someone you know who is farther along in their grief.

It is more than acceptable to ask someone who has suffered loss, and is far enough along to offer perspective, what was helpful to them in their grief so that YOU (not they) may minister to your hurting friend. Be careful not to try and force a relationship on these two. (See below.)

Not that

1. Do not tell them you know how it feels.

Do not convince yourself that you know how they are feeling, because I hope to God you do not. Otherwise, you may inadvertently communicate that your dog dying could possibly compare to their child dying. Or your child going away to college or to serve in the armed forces is in any way the same thing. So just do not say, "I know how you feel because..."

2. Do not say this was God's will.

Even if the person suffering trusts that God is Sovereign, they are struggling with anger at God for not doing something to save their loved one. If God opens the door for you to encourage them by reminding them of His character, consider saying, "This is so hard. I know you know God's character, so I am sure that can make it even more difficult to consider why He would want to take your beloved one to be with Him, instead of leaving them on this Earth for us all to be blessed longer here."

3. Do not feel compelled to come up with any plausible explanation.

The sufferer will be replaying how and why it happened over and over in the weeks, months, and years to come. It serves no good purpose for you to pose the question or offer your own ill-conceived conclusion in the immediate aftermath. That may make you feel better but does not provide any comfort to the hurting. When they are ready, they may reach out to you. If so, just listen and hold their hand. You do not have to figure anything out for them.

4. Do not talk about your own hurts.

Everyone hurts. There is enough suffering in the world for everyone to feel affected by it. Some hurt more than you and some less. This is not the time for you to think you will help them by telling them you hurt too. You can show sympathy and even empathy, but do not presume to compare hurts. This communicates you are looking for them to minister to you.

5. Do not force someone on them who has been through the same thing.

You find yourself hurting for this person who is suffering. You do not know how it feels personally, but you know someone who does. So of course the two should meet and be fast friends; forcing them together like a matchmaking service will surely be beneficial to all involved. NO. You are at a loss, and you just really want to do something. Your motivation is good, but this rarely works. It just needs to happen more naturally or even super-naturally. (See the chapter on recycled comfort.) God wants the one who is farther along in their grief to minister to those who have suffered in the same way. Do trust He will bring it about in His time. He has the power to do so.

6. Do not ask them how they are doing.

Sadly, even though I know better, I continue to do this. Even though I know they are doing awful and are just trying to get through the day, I will sometimes forget how unhelpful it is to ask a hurting person how they are doing. When the words come out, I wish I could take them back. Sometimes I can recover with, "I am so sorry, do not feel like you have to answer that". They may laugh nervously, or they say it's okay when we both know it's not. The point is, we will continue to say the wrong things even with the best of intentions. Try to recover if you can, and try to do better next time.

Ask questions they can answer with a simple yes or no. Instead of how are you doing, you could ask, Are you getting any sleep? Are you able to eat anything? Do you feel like going for a walk? These questions are easy for them to answer, but still tell you how they are doing. In time, you may be able to ask more open-ended questions.

7. Do not be a pity friend.

You want to reach out because they are hurting, but if you were not friends before the loss, be careful that your motivation in being their friend now is not out of pity or curiosity, fact-gathering, gossiping, or nosiness. Kindness and compassion are great, but pity will only last so long and then it will get old. When the person who is already suffering loss realizes you did not really want to be their friend, but just had pity on them, the hurt will be that much greater. Basically, do not lavish them with overtures of friendship if your motivation is out of pity, curiosity, fact-gathering, gossiping, or nosiness. No one wants to be pitied.

This is not exhaustive. Let the Holy Spirit be your guide more than anything. Most people will see your motivation was good and will not be devastated by a misstep. Hopefully, practicing these will help you be more mindful of how to minister. It is a blessing to do so.

CHAPTER NINE

ETERNAL LIFE IS THE ONLY LIFE THAT MATTERS

The moment Nicholas placed his trust in Jesus Christ as his Lord and Savior, his Eternal Life began.[1] This is the life God planned for him since before the world was created.[2] I treasure this truth and it is certainly a comfort, but when Nicholas died and physically left this Earth, I wanted to know all about where he was. *What has happened to him? What is he doing? If only I could see him once more.* I knew Heaven was the link to this becoming a reality. I immersed myself in studying the topic. *What is Heaven really like and when can I go?* It is remarkable that it takes loss to get us to think eternally. The Lord's return cannot come quickly enough.[3]

A friend recommended *One Minute After You Die* by Edwin Lutzer,[4] and I would recommend this resource as well. It is a short read but packed with scriptural support for why I can be comforted knowing that if my loved one is a child of God, they are at Home with Jesus the moment they leave this Earth.[5] I do not grieve as those who have no hope.[6] The Blessed Hope truly is a lifeline.[7] I know I will see them again, and for all eternity. I am counting the days until the glorious reunion. I am jealous of those who are already there.[8] To live is Christ and to die is gain resonates much more clearly now.[9] I tell the Lord I am ready when He is.

The thing is, shouldn't I already be thinking and living this way? If He is my Father, shouldn't I want to know Him and long to be with Him?[10] I should not feel at home here. I am not of this world. I am living as a resident alien.[11] My work is to do His will for as long as He wills it.[12] He numbered my days here when He formed me in my mother's womb and appointed the time of my departure from this Earth.[13] This should give me a sense of peace, knowing God is in control. He has a Sovereign plan.[14]

So why don't I live like I believe it? Why do I choose the trappings of this life over the next one? I make earthly things an idol, as if anything here could be better than what awaits. I like the idea of Heaven, but it can wait. Right up until... it can't, and it can't wait when someone I love more than myself lives there and not here. Then all of a sudden, Heaven can't wait. But isn't Someone I love more than myself already in Heaven?[15]

God used physical death to put a longing in my heart that should have already been there to get me to think with an eternal perspective. To look up instead of out. Even though it doesn't feel like it in the suffering, my life here is a vapor.[16] I do not understand God's Sovereign Plan that He ordained before the world began.[17] I don't know all the reasons He gave Nicholas a short physical life. I do trust Him. He has proven Himself over and over in His faithful, loving care. He gave His own Son so mine could live.[18] I cannot stay angry at the One who could have saved my son in this life, but chose instead to provide the Way to give him Eternal Life in the next one. He is not asking me to do anything He has not done Himself.

Thankfulness for Eternal Life

breaks the bond of anger and

binds it with cords of hope.

If I believe this, I am not sad for the one who went on to be with the Lord. I am sad for myself because I miss their presence here and must figure out life here without them. Their absence is a great loss, but I can learn not to wish them back. I have hope to not only join them, but also to live forever in sweet communion with our brothers and sisters, worshipping our Triune God—the Father, Son, and Holy Spirit.[19]

Eric and I shared the Gospel of Jesus Christ with our children from birth. Nicholas also heard this Good News at church and from other family members. So, it was not a surprise that he recognized he was a sinner and needed a Savior at an early age. Even so, we tried to put him off by saying how good it was that he wanted to follow Jesus. We did not use the words, "ask Jesus in your heart" to share the Gospel, but on five different occasions, Nicholas came home proclaiming he had done this.

By His Spirit, God had been drawing Nicholas to Himself for quite some time as truth was being revealed. We were using Christmas ornaments that share the truth of the Gospel by explaining the names of Jesus. On December 15, 2002, God used *Jesus as The Door* to completely illuminate Nicholas's understanding. John 10:9 says, "I am the door; if anyone enters by Me, he will be saved and will go in and out and find pasture" (ESV).

We could see understanding wash over him as he exclaimed, "Ohhhhhh! I get it." Then as he was saying his prayers at bedtime, when we tried to question him and maybe put him off a bit to make sure he really understood, he would not have it. He had to ask Jesus Christ to save him. He got on his knees, bowed his head, folded his hands, and quietly whispered a prayer to the Lord. When he opened his eyes he hopped into bed with a peaceful smile on his face, as if to say, "There, now that's settled."

Shortly after this, he was driving us crazy to get baptized. This went on for several months until we finally relented. I do not know if we were right to put him off. We wanted to have some assurance that he really understood what he was doing. Later as a teen, he had some rebellion that did not last long. Then six weeks before he died, he went to a discipleship weekend at church and came home with a renewed devotion to Jesus Christ as Lord that he could verbalize and articulate. There was also a noticeable difference in his priorities, respect, and obedience. This has been a great source of comfort to us in having assurance of seeing him again in Heaven. Praise be to God for this Blessed Hope.

If you do not have this hope, I implore you to read on. I want to share with you how you can know you have Eternal Life when your earthly life ceases to exist. None of us knows the number of our days. Life can change in an instant. We have great comfort in knowing that Nicholas had made this decision before he died.

God is the Creator of the universe, and it seemed good to Him to create man and woman in His image and give them a glorious place to live and worship Him.[20] Satan came along and told lies about God. They were very deceptive, and the woman believed them and disobeyed God. The man did not want to live without the woman, so he knowingly and willingly disobeyed God also.[21] Even though God removed them from the glorious place He had prepared for them, He promised to provide a way back to Himself.[22]

He can have nothing to do with sin; His character will not allow it, but because of His great love for us, He sent His only Son Jesus to be born of a virgin and live a perfect life with the purpose of paying the price for all sin.[23] The price was His blood shed as He died on a cross.[24] He took what we deserved and put it on Himself so we could live.[25] When God looks on us, He sees our account as paid in full.[26] The Good News does not stop there. Jesus Christ conquered death when He rose from the dead.[27] His resurrection is what gives us a Blessed Hope to be reunited with loved ones who have placed their trust in Christ.[28]

If you believe that Jesus's death was sufficient to pay the price for your sin, that it was not anything you could do yourself, and you ask Him to be Lord of your life, He will save you too.[29] This decision is the best decision you will ever make. It is the one that impacts your life for all of eternity and gives you assurance of where you will go when you die.[30] Christ will come back some day and re-establish His Kingdom on Earth as God intended before sin.[31] Until then, God gave us a beautiful gift, in the form of the Holy Spirit. He will guide and comfort and testify truth to our spirit.[32] We can live with hope as we await His return.[33]

I have just referenced a lot of places in the Bible that explain the hope of being saved and knowing how to have Eternal Life. If you are not familiar with how to find these references, or the task seems overwhelming, then I would encourage you to open a Bible, find the Gospel of John, and just start reading. Ask the Holy Spirit to guide you through the Truth contained therein. There are also many free Bible apps you could use or go online to BibleGateway.com.

It is my prayer that you make this decision right now if you have never done so. And send me a message that you have done it, so I can celebrate this life-changing Good News with you.[34]

CHAPTER TEN

A GLIMPSE OF HEAVEN

I just discussed in the last chapter how to know for sure you have Eternal Life, which is the premise for going to Heaven. It is important to view this chapter in light of that one. If you are not saved, then you are not able to look forward to Heaven and it offers no comfort to you, and I want each of you to have the Blessed Hope of eternity in Heaven.

God used death to give me a longing for eternity. First when my father died, and then it escalated when Nicholas died. Initially, I just wanted to see my daddy and Nicholas again. When I get there, I imagine Nicholas saying, "Oh, hi mom," like he has only been there about 15 minutes. Then as I gained understanding of what Heaven was like, I looked forward to going to Heaven as part of God's plan for my life. I only want to be on this Earth as long as God wills it. As soon as He finishes His work for me here, I am ready to go Home at any time, not only to be reunited with loved ones, but also to fulfill the perfect design God started in the Garden of Eden for His children and creation.

I am convinced when Christ returns to set up His Kingdom, it will look much like the Garden of Eden. God's design is perfect. When He created the world and everything in it, He proclaimed it was good. Sin entered the world and broke everything. This put a chasm between us and a holy God who can have nothing to do with sin. God in His great love, made a way back to Himself by sending His Son to pay the price for my sin. So, when God looks at me as His child, He sees the Righteousness of Jesus Christ credited to my account.

Since I was saved, God has used the joys and sorrows of this life to make me more and more like Christ. This is called sanctification and continues in the life of the believer until they die or Christ returns. I have already shared with you Erwin Lutzer's book, *One Minute After You Die*, to encourage you to know what happens to a believer the moment they die.

Would you like to know the rest of the story? What happens after that? What happens when Christ returns to set up His New Kingdom? My pastor, Tom Richter, calls this New Heaven New Earth, like it's all one word, "New-Heaven-New-Earth". He did a four-part sermon series on Heaven in July/ August 2018 that you can watch on Cullman First Baptist Church's website.[1]

He also references and recommends Randy Alcorn's book, *Heaven*[2] (2004, Tyndale House) to teach what the Bible says on the subject. This is an incredible and complete resource. I highly recommend it as well.

In the introduction, Alcorn grabbed my attention by helping me understand the truth about Heaven that dramatically changed my perspective on how to live this life with a view to the next. He tells a story of a swimmer, Florence Chadwick (1918-1995), who successfully swam the English Channel—23 miles round trip—in 1951. And then in 1952, she wanted to swim the Pacific, 21 miles from Catalina Island to the shore of California.[3] The weather was foggy and chilly, and after swimming 20.5 miles in 15 plus hours, she was physically and emotionally exhausted. Her mother was in the safety boat and tried to encourage her to finish, that the end was close, but she stopped and begged to be pulled out. At a news conference the next day she said that if she could have seen the shore, which was only a half mile away, she thinks she could have finished. All she could see was the fog.

If we could see through the fog of pain and heartache, what awaits will not only outweigh the suffering here, but also count for glory there. Alcorn says, "Picturing our eternal home in our mind's eye will comfort and energize us."[4]

If you want to know with confidence that what comes next for God's children is an exciting adventure where we use our gifts and abilities to bring Him glory in a physical place that Jesus is preparing, then I encourage you to read on.

Revelation 13:6 says Satan slanders God's person, people, and place because he was evicted from Heaven. He wants us to believe lies about the home he was kicked out of and can never return, but we are entitled to go there and stay there. The reason we have an impoverished view of Heaven is because Satan convinces us it is a boring, unearthly existence that we won't enjoy or even recognize. The truth is, Heaven is not beyond what we can envision if our imagination is biblically inspired.[5] Satan delights in keeping us from enjoying the life God planned for us. It is important to be aware of his devices. One major scheme of the enemy is to twist God's Word. This may lead us to not handle Scripture accurately.

People often misquote Scripture, leave out essential parts, or take it out of context when looking to the Bible to see what God reveals to us.[6] First Corinthians 2:9 is one such passage that is incorrectly thought to refer to the wonders of Heaven: "What no eye has seen, nor ear heard, nor the heart of man imagined, what God has prepared for those who love him." If you read on, verse 10 says, "These things God has revealed to us through the Spirit. For the Spirit searches everything, even the depths of God." This verse and those following teach that the wisdom of God is made known through His Word and the Spirit by revelation, inspiration, and illumination.[7]

Deuteronomy 29:29 is another example, "The secret things belong to the LORD our God". If you finish the rest of the verse, "...but the things that are revealed belong to us and to our children forever, that we may do all the words of this law," you will see God wants us to know what He has revealed to us in His Word.[8] "Seek the things that are above, where Christ is seated at the right hand of God" (Colossians 3:1) is a direct command for us to keep on in the process of seeking Heaven. We fix our minds so much on this Earth, we do not even recognize the desire for Heaven that God put in our hearts.[9]

In order to have a biblical worldview, Alcorn says we must have a sense of the three phases of Earth's history: the past in Genesis 1 and 2, the present in Genesis 3 through Revelation 20, and the future in Revelation 21 and 22.[10] We live in between the Garden of Eden and Paradise.[11] Isaiah, Peter, and John (in the book of Revelation) all speak of the New Heaven and New Earth God has promised for His children. If we look more closely at Isaiah 60 and compare it to Revelation 21, God isn't going to abandon the first plan; He is going to redeem and restore the Earth so that nothing impure will enter it.[12] The current Earth will be set on fire to purify it so that it is once again inhabitable when Heaven comes to join it. Thus, the New Heaven New Earth will be complete and the curse will be lifted.[13] The Earth can only be delivered from the curse of sin by being redeemed and resurrected.[14] The power of Christ's resurrection is enough not only to remake us, but also every inch of the universe. Creation is eagerly awaiting to follow us in being changed to the glorious nature God intended, much like it was in the Garden of Eden. Alcorn says, "It is no coincidence that the first two chapters of the Bible (Genesis 1-2) begin with the creation of the heavens and the Earth, and the last two chapters (Revelation 21-22) begin with the re-creation of the heavens and the Earth. All that was lost at the beginning will be restored at the end, and far more will be added besides."[15] The reference for understanding the future of Earth's destruction by fire is its past destruction by the flood, a cleansing judgment to eliminate sin which will immediately be followed by its resurrection to new life.[16]

In other words, God uses water and fire to judge, but also to purify and make the Earth ready to be reinhabited. His original plan was not a failure.[17] God brings to perfection what He started in the Garden of Eden. He promises His children a forever, physical Home with all of the beauty and none of the ugliness that sin and death created. It's a place of love and hospitality filled with the familiarity of the things and people we cherish. Enjoying our favorite music, reading a good book, walking in the park, riding bikes, inviting friends over to barbecue, and savoring a cup of coffee as the sun rises are all things we enjoy because we are human, not because we are sinners. These are but a glimpse of the greater life to come.

C.S. Lewis (1898-1963) often wrote on the subject of Heaven. Many who have influenced me have also been influenced by Lewis's writings. So, I feel validated to look to his writings for encouragement as well. Lewis was grieved by the loss of his wife and spoke much about what awaits us in the future. He said in his book, *Mere Christianity*, "If I find in myself a desire which no experience in this world can satisfy, the most probable explanation is that I was made for another world."[18] I am looking forward to this so much I am homesick, but what does this mean for us presently?

Our present life can be described in terms of the "already and not yet."[19] Christ already defeated death with His own death and resurrection, assuring the resurrection of man and the Earth. This loosened the grip Satan has on the Earth currently; but it is not until Satan is cast into the lake of fire, that he will be unable to rule, influence, or touch the Earth again. Christ has already defeated Satan, but the full scope of the victory has not yet been manifested on Earth. Ephesians 1 says God placed all things under His feet and appointed Christ to be head over everything. He is the Sovereign Ruler, and yet, it is only when Christ returns that Satan will be bound. There will be a war and Christ and His Bride will be victorious.

I do not imagine this battle taking very long for the King of Kings. What is gloriously fascinating is we are at least along for the ride, if not engaged in fighting as well, perhaps something akin to the battle in *The Lion, the Witch, and the Wardrobe*, by C.S. Lewis.[20] It's part of the *Chronicles of Narnia* series. Eric read these books to us when Nicholas and Drew were children. The movie has also become a favorite in the Fillinger household. This is a fictional series, but Lewis is a master storyteller and uses imagery from Scripture to enhance our imaginations. In the above mentioned scene, the Witch is gaining ground and defeat appears imminent. Unbeknownst to those engaged in battle, the Lion is on the move.

The Lion had willingly died in place of the traitor, Edward. He came back to life, and said, "...when a willing victim who had committed no treachery was killed in the traitor's stead, the

Table would crack and Death itself would start working backward."[21] He arrives and it takes but one powerful roar to turn the tide. Narnia is set to right, and the victors take their place as rulers in the beautiful city.

Ponder for a moment what it means that death is conquered. Death does not have the final say. Who are we to grieve without hope? We know the truth and it is a blessing. The days seem long as we tarry here, but they are but a vapor in comparison to what awaits. Our Eternal Life seems to begin when we become saved, but God had our days planned out beforehand. Death doesn't win. I preach to myself this sermon of the Blessed Hope often.[22] It encourages me to view today in light of what I know to be true: Glory days are coming!

Our redemption and resurrection are contingent upon Christ's resurrection. The resurrection is essential to our faith.[23] Had Christ not risen, we are still dead in our sins, our faith in the future is futile, and we should be pitied more than anyone.[24] Christ conquered death and the power of sin when He was raised from the dead. Our sin is buried with Him and our new life raised with His, partially now and completely in the future.[25]

We learn much of what our resurrected and glorified bodies will be like by looking at His, as ours will be like His.[26] Christ walked the Earth after His death and resurrection in an earthly, human body. He proclaimed He was not a ghost when He met with His disciples and they saw the nail prints in His hands, and He walked on the Emmaus Road conversing with others. He and His disciples met on the shore, started a fire, and cooked breakfast, resuming their relationship where they had left off. This tells us that we will still be ourselves but with an upgrade, unable to sin and, therefore, able to see Christ with unveiled face in all His Glory.[27]

No one on present Earth can look upon the Glory of God and live.[28] Yet, when we are glorified, we will see Him in all His Glory and live with Him.[29] May we not be tempted to say it's too much to imagine, because imagining it is part of the anticipation that keeps us encouraged to press on.

Anticipating Resurrection Life also has practical implications for the present.[30] Our service is carried over. Nothing we do for the Lord is lost or wasted. When Moses prayed, "Establish the work of our hands" in Psalm 90:17, establish meant to make permanent. Righteous works follow us to Heaven. This excites me to be busy doing Kingdom work. What do I do on this Earth that has eternal significance? That is what will last.

Hopefully, your foundational understanding of Heaven is starting to solidify. If you are like me, though, you have some questions.

What will the resurrected Earth be like?[31] Will it be an Edenic Paradise? This life gives but a glimpse of the next one. Don't be fooled into thinking you can have your best life now if you are a child of God. Consider the Grand Canyon, Amazon River, The Alps—all are just a whisper of the glory to come. All of the old Earth that matters will be drawn into Heaven, to be part of the New Earth. The Garden of Eden was just the starting point. According to Revelation 21, the onyx in Eden will be in the foundations of New Jerusalem's walls in a literal geographical location. Hebrews 11 says God is the architect. This Great City is the capital of God's Kingdom and home to the King of Kings. As His heirs, we will be free to explore all the great wonders, not only inside the city walls, but also outside of them. The curse devastated the sea and contaminated the oceans, but the River of Life will flow through the Great City and on each side of the river will stand the Tree of Life from which we will eat freely for nourishment and healing, according to Revelation 2 and 22.

In *The Weight of Glory*, C. S. Lewis puts it like this, "We want something else which can hardly be put into words—to be united with the beauty we see, to pass into it, to receive it into ourselves, to bathe in it, to become part of it."[32]

What will our lives be like?[33] Will we be ourselves? Isaiah 66:22 says, "For as the new heavens and the new Earth that I make shall remain before me, says the LORD, so shall your offspring and your name remain." Our names are written in the Lamb's Book of Life, according to Revelation 20:15. Jesus called Abraham, Isaac, and Jacob by the same name in Heaven as they had on Earth, according to Matthew 8, denoting a distinct identity and demonstrating they remained the same people without the bad parts. Who you are here in your most Jesus-like state is a taste of who you will be in Heaven. On New Earth, for the first time you will be the person God created you to be with godly desires and pure motives, expressing emotion with tears of joy. Our hope of living without sin is part of the gospel message and will finally be realized.

What will we know and learn?[34] We will see more clearly but will not know everything. Only God is omniscient. We will live in a process of deepening appreciation of God's greatness as forever learners and innovators. Intellectual curiosity is a blessing. Our daily lives will also be filled with work we enjoy, relaxation and rest, joyful praise, and fellowship with one another and Jesus, who desires our company.

What else will we do?[35] God called us to adventure and creativity. He is the inventor of laughter and wit. We will be reigning and ruling with King Jesus and helping Him run the universe with unlimited resources. Arts, entertainment, and sports? Yes, please. Along with music and dance and drama. God created and values a child-like spirit.[36] These things are not part of the curse; we are given gifts for the common good. We will be satisfied, laugh, and leap for joy.[37]

What will our relationships be like?[38] Relationships here are hard because of selfishness and pride. Without the presence of sin, I can anticipate living in perfect harmony with those I love and who love me. Human marriage will end, but not deep and meaningful relationships. Marriage here prepares us for the perfect union of Christ with His Bride, the Church. The Church is made up of people from every tribe and nation (Daniel 7 and Revelation 7). We will meet new people and discover new cultures, enjoying the diversity while living in peace.

All of this sounds like a dream, but we have full assurance this dream will become a reality when Christ returns to set up His Kingdom on Earth. In the meantime, what does this mean for us now as we struggle through this life? One of the biggest encouragements from the last section of Alcorn's *Heaven*, "To Live in Light of Heaven" was this: "If we see ourselves in heaven with Christ, we will worship and serve Him here and now, creating ripples in heaven's waters that will extend for all eternity."[39]

With a scripture-enhanced imagination, we can reorient ourselves to Heaven as our Home; Eden is in our blood.[40] Heaven is the source of our optimism because it is the realm we were made for. It is what makes us long for the Resurrection. Meditating on Heaven is a great pain reliever which encourages us to pray for Christ's Return. Everything that happens here is getting us ready. We will reap in eternity what we have planted in this life.[41]

Setting our minds on Heaven is a discipline we must learn because it liberates us from the shallow hopelessness of life centered on a fallen and failing world. Living righteous lives here pays off in eternity and for eternity, and gives a different perspective here and now. The suffering will not last, but the glory will. It helps us focus our energy on what lasts and not worry about that which has no eternal significance. "O God you are my God; earnestly I seek you; my soul thirsts for you; my flesh faints for you; as in a dry and weary land where there is no water" (Psalm 63:1).

It won't be long now until our thirst is quenched. Because of Christ's righteousness in us, soon we will see God's face and behold His Glory.[42]

It will astound us and be our greatest joy, the joy by which all others will be measured. We will know God and never grow weary of knowing Him more as He fills the universe with His Glory. He will dwell among us and we will live together in the same Home. Wherever we go, we will enjoy the complete manifestation of God's presence.

The best example from my personal life of someone who lived in light of eternity was my father-in-law. We call him Pops. I have never seen anyone more ready to go Home than Pops. He had been dealing with chronic lymphocytic leukemia (CLL) for 15 years. It was well-controlled and he was pretty much able to do what he wanted right up until the end. It was important to him to remain very productive. I would call him and ask what he was doing and his reply was always the same, "I'm working J woman. I'm always working." He loved to be busy doing the work God had for him to do.

But then he started getting more tired. He just didn't have the energy to do the things he wanted to do anymore. He was even taking naps. He would still get up before the crack of dawn but would need to lie down a couple of hours later. This was unusual since he spoke out against "Logdoggers". He had made it clear from the time he was diagnosed with CLL, he only wanted to be here on this Earth as long as God had productive work for him to do.

When he contracted COVID, he initially refused to even get tested. I tried to reason with him, that COVID could be fatal for him and Beammie (my mother-in-love has multiple sclerosis). He responded with, "I'm ready to die!" To which I asked, "What about Beammie?" He said, "She's ready to die too." I told him that was not up to him. I called Eric and asked him to talk to Pops. He got tested the next day. Beammie tested positive the following day. The day after that, they both were able to receive an infusion.

Beammie recovered well and Pops's initial response was good too, but then he needed an inhaler, then home oxygen. With each treatment he would start to get better, and then a couple days later would get worse. When he was hospitalized, I poked him in the chest and told him he had to fight this. He sighed deeply and said okay, but I could see he didn't have much fighting left in him. He eventually needed BiPAP in order to breathe.

At this time, he could only have one visitor. My husband Eric checked on him every day and felt the weight of making decisions and informing the family. Pops got to the point where he was going to need a ventilator in order to keep his oxygenation at a sustainable level. He told Eric emphatically, "Do not put me on a ventilator!" Eric tried to explain to him that this was the next step in the treatment protocol, and it may only be for a couple weeks so his lungs had a chance to heal. Pops remained adamant that he did not want to go on a ventilator. He said, "Why would you want to keep me from Heaven?"

Pops had also been dealing with some bladder control. While he was in the hospital, a urologist friend was consulted. The ultrasound showed Pops had numerous tumors in his bladder. It seemed Pops had known something like this was going on for a while.

The day before he died, the urologist rounded on him and noticed a change in his breathing. He tried to call Eric but couldn't reach him because he was in surgery. Dr. Braswell was not just our urologist; he is also our friend. So, when he couldn't reach Eric, he called me and said, "Julie, Eric needs to go check on his father." Pops's struggle to breathe was worsening and the decision was made to call the Palliative Care Team.

Everything was happening so quickly for us, but right on schedule in God's timing. We informed the family that Pops may not live much longer. Eric's brother, Rod, had just been here and was able to see and spend some time with his father—precious moments he now greatly treasures.

Our son Drew and niece Emily only lived a few hours away and were able to come the next morning. Beammie, Eric, and I met them at the hospital. You could have more visitors when you are under the care of the Palliative Care Team.

The five of us were surrounding Pops's bed, trying to grasp what was happening. Pops said he wasn't waiting and motioned with his hand to get this show on the road. He was ready, but we were not. The Palliative Care Team would come at 2:30 pm to remove the BiPAP. It became obvious he wasn't going to live much longer and the team made him more comfortable.

We prayed and sang hymns and worshipped God, thanking Him for Pops's life and asking Him for mercy and peace. After a short time, Pops raised his hands with the little strength he had and peace washed over his countenance. He then breathed his last breath. His time of death was 3:46 pm, or 15:46 in military time. He had gone Home.

It didn't take long for the significance of the time of death to jolt Eric and me in awestruck wonder. Nicholas's personal record for a 5K was 15:46. That was what he ran his last race before he died. He had broken the school record with that time. We assumed he would have many more opportunities to break it again and again. Only he didn't. That would be his last. Many of his friends and teammates had tattooed that time on their bodies in memory of him.

Now for us, the time took on a different significance. It was as if God was saying Pops died at His appointed time. He had finished the race and Nicholas was there at the finish line to greet him, "Hey Pops, I'm glad you're here. I think you're going to like it. Now let's go see Jesus. I think He wants to give you a hug, just like He did me."

We have peace knowing my daddy, Nicholas, and Pops are in the presence of their Lord. It takes courage to continue to live in light of this Truth, but it won't be too much longer. May we press on and rest in God's goodness and faithfulness until we go Home or Christ returns, whichever comes first.

ENDNOTES

Chapter One
1. 2 Kings 20
2. Luke 22:42

Chapter Two
1. Exodus 20:3
2. Revelation 4:11
3. "courage." *Merriam-Webster.com*. Merriam-Webster, 2022. Web. 9 September 2022.
4. Psalm 40:1-3
5. Romans 8:16, 17
6. Hebrew 13:5
7. Romans 8:28
8. Psalm 126:5,6; Isaiah 35:10

Chapter Three
1. Wayne Grudem, "The Essential Nature of Man", Systematic Theology 2nd Edition. Grand Rapids: Zondervan 1994, 2020.
   Joel R. Beeke, Paul M. Smalley, "The Constitution of Man", Reformed Systematic Theology, Volume 2, Man and Christ. Wheaton: Crossway 2020. Downloads.biblicaltraining.org. Louis Berkhof, "The Constitutional Nature of Man", Systematic Theology. Grand Rapids: Eerdmans Pub. Co., 1949. (accessed September 30, 2022).
2. Ecclesiastes 11:5, Deuteronomy 29:29, 1 Corinthians 2:9,10

3. Spiros Zodhiates, The Complete Word Study Dictionary New Testament. Chattanooga: AMG International 1992, revised 1993.

4. Grudem, 600-617; Beeke, 230-264; Berkhof, 206-218.

5. Psalm 42

6. Psalm 40:1-3

7. Genesis 1:26 and 5:1,2; James 3:9; Psalm 139:17, Psalm78:41, 1 Corinthians 1:1

8. Romans 8:17, John 16:13

9. 1 Corinthians 2:10-14

10. Ephesians 6:11, 1 John 5:18

11. 1 Thessalonians 5:23

12. 1 Corinthians 15:57

13. Ephesians 1:13,14

14. David Depp, "It is Well with My Soul: Historical Origins of the Hymn and the Tune." YouTube, 10/27/2015. (accessed September 10, 2022) SpaffordHymn.com: The Original Hymn Manuscript. n.d. (accessed September 25, 2022) 14. Rev. Angus Stewart, "Horatio Spafford: Not Well With His Soul", CPRC.CO.UK. n.d. (accessed September 10, 2022)

15. Job 14:5 and Psalm 139:16

16. John 14:1-6

17. James 4:14

18. Revelation 22:20

19. Romans 8:18

20. 2 Corinthians 5:8

21. 1 Thessalonians 4:16,17

22. Genesis 1:31

23. Genesis 3:1-6

24. Matthew 25:34
25. Hebrews 12:1-3, 2 Timothy 2:8-13

Chapter Four

1. Matthew 28:18
2. Psalm 103:19, 135:6
3. Hebrews 11:1
4. 2 Corinthians 12:9, 10
5. 2 Samuel 11
6. 2 Samuel 12
7. Matthew 5:21-30
8. 2 Samuel 11:11
9. Leviticus 20:10
10. 2 Samuel 12:23
11. John 16:33
12. 2 Corinthians 4:7-18
13. Job 1
14. Job 2:3
15. John 9:1-7
16. Hebrews 9:15-28
17. Interview, Dr. Tom Richter, Cullman First Baptist Church, Cullman, AL. September 9, 2022.
18. 1 Samuel 13:14
19. Ezekiel 36:26-28
20. Romans 5:5-9
21. Romans 8:16
22. Psalm 6, 32, 38, 51, 143
23. 1 Peter 2:24, Hebrews 10:22
24. 1 Peter 5:10
25. Ephesians 6:10-18
26. 2 Chronicles 20:15
27. Psalm33:6
28. Galatians 2:20

29. 2 Corinthians 12:9,10
30. Psalm 91
31. Ephesians 4:32
32. Matthew 5:3
33. Ephesians 2:8, 9
34. 1 Corinthians 15
35. Colossians 3:1-3
36. John 15:4-9
37. 1 Corinthians 1:9

Chapter Five

1. Hebrews 11:1
2. Romans 8:11, Ephesians 1:18,19 and 3:20,21
3. Romans 8:16-18
4. Hebrews 2:14-18, 1 Peter 2:24 and 3:18
5. Elizabeth B. Brown, Surviving the Loss of a Child. Revell, Grand Rapids, 2010.
6. Edwin W. Lutzer, One Minute After You Die. Moody, Chicago, 1997.
7. Ecclesiastes 3:11
8. John14:26
9. John 16:13, Romans 8:5, Ezekiel 36:26,27
10. Lamentations 3:22, 23
11. Psalm 34:17,18 and 51:17, Isaiah 61:1-3, 1 Peter 4:19, 2 Thessalonians 2:16,17
12. 1 Thessalonians 4:13
13. Hebrews 4:16
14. Romans 8:18

Chapter Six

1. 1 Samuel 1:27,28
2. Exodus 20:3-6; 1 John 5:21
3. Isaiah 51:11
4. John 6:40

5. Isaiah 26:3,4; Isaiah 41:10
6. Romans 8:28
7. 1 Thessalonians 2:12
8. Psalm 53:2, 1 Chronicles 28:9, Philippians 3:17
9. Philippians 3:17

Chapter Seven

1. Job 1 and 2
2. Psalm 69:15
3. Psalm 10:1
4. Ephesians 6:12
5. Psalm 6:3
6. Hebrews 4:16
7. Matthew 18:20
8. 2 Corinthians 12:9,10
9. Romans 8:38,39
10. Hebrews 7:25
11. John 14:13
12. 1 Peter 5:6
13. Ann VosKamp, One Thousand Gifts. Zondervan, Grand Rapids, 2010.
14. Colossians 3:15-17
15. John 3:16
16. 1 Thessalonians 4:13-18
17. Ephesians 2:4,5
18. Romans 5:5
19. 2 Corinthians 5:6-9
20. Job 2:1-6
21. Psalm 40:1-3
22. Sally Lloyd-Jones, The Jesus Storybook Bible. Zonderkidz, Grand Rapids, 2007.
23. John 16:13

Chapter Nine

1. John 11:25, 26
2. Ephesians 1:4-6
3. Revelation 22:20
4. Erwin W. Lutzer, One Minute After You Die. Moody, Chicago, 1997.
5. 2 Corinthians 5:8
6. 1 Thessalonians 4:13-18
7. Titus 2:13
8. Philippians 3:20
9. Philippians 1:21
10. Matthew 23:9
11. John 15:19, 1 Peter 2:11
12. Ephesians 2:10, James 4:15
13. Psalm139:16, Hebrews 9
14. Ephesians 1:11
15. Luke 11:2
16. James 4:14
17. Titus 1:2
18. John 3:16
19. John 14
20. Genesis 1
21. Genesis 3:1-7
22. Genesis 3:8-19
23. Luke 1:35; Matthew 1:22, 23; John 3:16, 17; 2 Corinthians 5:21; Romans 5:8; Ephesians 2:4,5
24. Galatians 4:4, 1 Peter 2:24, Hebrews 9:22 & 12:2, Ephesians 1:7
25. Philippians 2:6,7; Galatians 3:13
26. Romans 6:23, Hebrews 10:10
27. 1 Peter 1:3; John 11:25, 26; 1 Corinthians 15:55; Romans 6:9

28. 1 Thessalonians 4:13-15
29. Ephesians 2:8,9; Romans 10:9,10
30. John 10:28, 1 John 5:11-13
31. Hebrews 9:28, 1 Thessalonians 4:16-18, John 14:3
32. Ephesians 1:13, John 14:26, John 16:7, Romans 8:9
33. John 10:10, Romans 15:13
34. julie@juliefillinger.com

Chapter Ten

1. Tom Richter, "Heaven", Cullman First Baptist Church, streamed live July 22 – August 12, 2018, Cullman, AL. www.cullmanfbc.com.
2. Randy Alcorn, Heaven. Carol Stream, IL: Tyndale, 2004.
3. Florence Chadwick sermon illustration. https://bible.sabda.org/illustration.php?id=5927
4. Alcorn, Heaven, xx.
5. Ibid, 15.
6. Ibid, 18.
7. John Macarthur, The Macarthur Study Bible. Nashville: Thomas Nelson, 2006.
8. Alcorn, Heaven, 19.
9. Ibid, 20-21.
10. Ibid, 81-85.
11. Ibid, 85-87.
12. Ibid, 20, 88-99.
13. Ibid, 101-104.
14. Ibid, 125-133.
15. Ibid, 132
16. Ibid, 154-157.
17. Ibid, 159-167.

18. C.S. Lewis, Mere Christianity. New York: Macmillan, 1972.
19. Alcorn, Heaven, 105-108.
20. C.S. Lewis, The Lion, The Witch, and The Wardrobe. Grand Rapids: Zonderkidz, 2005.
21. Ibid, Chapter 15.
22. Titus 2:12,13.
23. Alcorn, Heaven, 111-116.
24. 1 Corinthians 15:17-19.
25. Romans 6:4.
26. 1 John 3:2, Philippians 3:20, 21.
27. Alcorn, Heaven, 117-121
28. Exodus 33:20.
29. Revelation 22:3,4.
30. Alcorn, Heaven, 133-134.
31. Ibid, 241-275.
32. C.S. Lewis, The Weight of Glory and Other Addresses, Revised and expanded edition. New York: Macmillan, 1980.
33. Alcorn, Heaven, 281-316.
34. Ibid, 317-321.
35. Ibid, 329-336, 409-429.
36. Mark 10:14, 15.
37. 1 Corinthians 12:7, Luke 6:21-25.
38. Alcorn, Heaven, 337-383.
39. Ibid, 193.
40. Ibid, 455-473.
41. Galatians 6:7,8
42. Alcorn, Heaven, 171-187.

ABOUT
KHARIS PUBLISHING:

Kharis Publishing, an imprint of Kharis Media LLC, is a leading Christian and inspirational book publisher based in Aurora, Chicago metropolitan area, Illinois. Kharis' dual mission is to give voice to under-represented writers (including women and first-time authors) and equip orphans in developing countries with literacy tools. That is why, for each book sold, the publisher channels some of the proceeds into providing books and computers for orphanages in developing countries so that these kids may learn to read, dream, and grow. For a limited time, Kharis Publishing is accepting unsolicited queries for nonfiction (Christian, self-help, memoirs, business, health and wellness) from qualified leaders, professionals, pastors, and ministers. Learn more at: https://kharispublishing.com/